Eucharistic Presidency

GS 1248

Eucharistic Presidency

A Theological Statement
by the House of Bishops
of the General Synod

CHURCH HOUSE PUBLISHING
Church House, Great Smith Street, London SW1P 3NZ

Church House Publishing,
Church House,
Great Smith Street,
London SW1P 3NZ

ISBN 0-7151-3804-9

Published 1997 for the General Synod of the Church of England by Church House Publishing

Cover design by Sarah Hopper

Printed in England by The Cromwell Press Ltd, Melksham, Wiltshire.

Contents

Foreword

In July 1994 the General Synod requested a statement from the House of Bishops about '. . . the theology of the Eucharist and about the respective roles of clergy and laity within it'.

This Report is the House's response to that request. As the Bishop of Ely's Preface makes clear it is the fruit of very full consideration by the House of the issues raised by the General Synod's request for it.

We offer our Report for study and reflection within the Church.

On behalf of the House of Bishops
✠ *George Cantuar*
Chairman

April 1997

Preface

It is the special responsibility of the bishops of the Church to maintain and further the unity of the Church, to uphold its discipline, and to guard its faith. But guardianship is never merely a defensive exercise. As the Preface to the Declaration of Assent makes clear, the Church is called upon to proclaim the faith afresh in each generation. Each generation has its own questions, and it is a legitimate part of the bishops' task to foster reverent and scholarly enquiry and the testing of inherited traditions, and actively to participate in argument on disputed questions.

The riskiness of such enquiry was already robustly faced by the Anglican bishops assembled one hundred years ago at the Lambeth Conference. In relation to the controversies attending the critical study of the Bible they wrote in their encyclical:

> A faith which is always or often attended by a secret fear that we dare not inquire lest inquiry should lead us to results inconsistent with what we believe, is already infested with a disease which may soon destroy it (*The First Lambeth Conferences*, SPCK, 1920, p.188f).

Therefore, although from the sixteenth century Anglican writers have defended the inherited Catholic tradition that the celebration of the Eucharist should be presided over by an ordained priest or presbyter, it is by no means illegitimate to ask – and the question has now arisen – how firmly grounded this tradition is in theology and pastoral practice.

When the House of Bishops received the request of the General Synod for a theological statement about the Eucharist and the respective roles of the clergy and laity within it, it took steps to invite a number of theologians of different denominations and theological traditions to help with the enquiry. These included scholars known to be in favour of lay presidency. The House also asked two further theologians to consider the invited contributions, a range of ecumenical agreed statements and literature from other parts of the Anglican Communion, and to prepare a draft for the House to consider. The House of Bishops is, therefore, deeply indebted to very many who have generously drawn on their knowledge and experience in assisting the House in the discharge of its responsibilities. In particular it thanks the Reverend Dr Jeremy Begbie, Vice-Principal of Ridley Hall, Cambridge.

The draft was presented and given its first revision at a meeting of all the bishops. It was sent for consideration by the Faith and Order Advisory Group. Then it was further discussed in regional groups of bishops. It was finally amended and agreed at a meeting of the House of Bishops. This thorough procedure is an indication both of the importance which the bishops attach to the question, and of their determination to take with full seriousness their task of maintaining the unity of the Church and of guarding its faith.

There are five main chapters, and a brief conclusion, in this work. Chapter 1 deals with the state of the 'lay presidency' question; Chapter 2 expounds the Church of the triune God as the context of a variety of ministries; Chapter 3 describes the Church's ministry and ministries, and the complementary roles of clergy and laity; Chapter 4 deals with the Eucharist and the president of the Eucharist; Chapter 5 considers nine arguments about 'lay presidency'.

It is apparent from this that Chapters 2, 3 and 4 contain the heart of the matter. On the basis of an interpretation of the theological context in which the question arises, these chapters move theologically (as they should) from God to Church and from there to ministry and sacrament.

At the risk of unduly condensing the exposition of these themes, attention is drawn to the conclusion expressed in Chapter 4 (4.43):

> The eucharistic president is to be a sign and the focus of the unity, holiness, catholicity and apostolicity of the Church, and the one who has primary responsibility for ensuring that the Church's four marks are expressed, actualised and made visible in the eucharistic celebration.

In this brief statement the contents of the first four chapters are brought together – presidency, the Church, the ministry and the eucharistic celebration.

A trinitarian understanding of the Church sheds light on how a community of worship and mission is brought into being and how it is sustained. In it the Holy Spirit is at work in maintaining its unity with diversity and anticipating the fellowship of the kingdom in the last days. The four marks of the Church, its oneness, catholicity and apostolicity, make up a pattern of relationships 'engendered by the Church's sharing in the triune communion of God (2.24).

In the context of such a Church the ordained ministry is best understood 'as a gift of God to his Church to promote, release and clarify all other ministries in such a way that they can exemplify and sustain the four marks of the Church' (3.26).

The Eucharist, in turn, is a trinitarian feast, constitive of the Church through the Holy Spirit. In showing forth the death of the Lord until he comes, it expresses, actualises and makes visible the identity of the Church in its four marks. The whole people of God celebrates the feast. In it there is a proper differentiation of role which is nevertheless not a ranking of persons in their relation to God. The ministry of word, sacrament and pastoral oversight are properly united in eucharistic presidency, which not merely sustains the local church but also points to the Church universal.

Chapters 1–4 contain a theological response to a precise and particular request to elucidate eucharistic theology and the respective roles of the clergy and laity within it. The statement is not intended to a be a complete account of priestly ministry. Nor is it a step by step refutation of arguments advanced in favour of lay presidency. None the less Chapter 5 briefly considers nine responses, consistent with the theological position advanced in Chapters 2, 3 and 4, to those who offer theological justification for lay presidency. The conclusion is that we believe there are strong theological arguments for sustaining the tradition we have inherited, set out in Canon B12 (that the person who presides at the Eucharist must be an episcopally ordained priest).

This conclusion has been reached within the urgent mission context and imperative faced by the Church in our day. That mission can never consist in the attempt 'to preserve, re-live, or replicate an ancient tradition in the present'. Rather through the power of the Holy Spirit we are summoned to fresh actualisations of the tradition, in fidelity to and continuity with apostolic faith, so that 'the truth of Christ is brought alive for the ever new situations with which the Church engages in its missionary calling' (2.28).

It is with that intention that we offer the statement which follows for study and reflection.

✠ STEPHEN ELY

(on behalf of the House of Bishops Theological Group)

1

Introduction

The immediate occasion of the statement

1.1   On July 10th 1994, in response to a Private Member's motion put forward by Mr Timothy Royle, General Synod approved an amended motion stating:

> That this Synod, while accepting that lay presidency at the Eucharist is incompatible with Anglican tradition, would welcome a statement from the House of Bishops about the theology of the Eucharist and about the respective roles of clergy and laity within it.

It should be stressed that this request is primarily for a *theological* statement. This means that although it may well be important to consider future arrangements for adequate eucharistic provision in the Church of England, and although this report may carry practical implications for such provision, it is not the purpose of this statement to recommend or press for any particular strategies in this regard. The principal aim is to highlight and engage with the major theological issues at stake in a theology of the Eucharist which pays special attention to the respective roles of clergy and laity.

'Lay,' 'clergy,' 'presidency', 'lay presidency' and 'local'

To begin with, some clarification of terms is necessary.

1.2.   Properly speaking, the word 'laity' applies to every baptised member of the Church, the people (*laos*) of God. The 'clergy' are those of the laity called by God and ordained by the Church to ministry in the orders of bishop, priest/presbyter or deacon.

1.3   The development of the term 'lay' to speak of a group distinguished from the ordained is usually traced to Clement of Rome who, towards the end of the first century AD, was referring to those not ordained as deacon or presbyter.[1] It is often pointed out that this use of the word 'lay' obscures the fact that the whole Church is the laity and thus encourages 'clericalisation' within the Church; that is, a tendency to conceive the ordained as essentially separate from and superior to the rest of the people of God. It is beyond doubt that the Church has often succumbed to clericalisation and that the recovery of the conviction that the entire membership of the Church celebrates the Eucharist is one of the key requirements for providing an adequate account of the roles of the various participants at the Eucharist. However, for the sake of clarity, unless otherwise stated, we shall understand *'laity'* as referring to *those baptised members of the Church who are not ordained to the threefold ministry of bishop, priest or deacon* and the *'clergy'* as referring to those who are so ordained.

the most contentious area with regard to roles: 'lay presidency'

1.4   The most contentious area of debate with regard to the roles of laity and clergy at the Eucharist is made explicit in the opening sentence of the motion: 'lay presidency'.

'presidency' is a word with a fluidity of meaning

1.5   'Presidency' is a word with a fluidity of meaning. Its first known relevant use, by Justin Martyr (second century), appears to refer to a leader with an ongoing role with respect to a particular congregation. Within the Church of England, the word has been used only recently. (*The Book of Common Prayer* (1662) (BCP) speaks of 'ministering' or 'administering' the sacrament.) The term 'president' was introduced in 1971 into the Series 3 eucharistic liturgy. The concept of presidency at the Eucharist was central to the 1975 General Synod Faith and Order Report, *The Theology of Ordination*.[2] The publication of *The Alternative Service Book 1980* (ASB) brought the word into common use.

the president presides over the whole service

1.6   What is entailed in presiding at the Eucharist is described in the ASB as follows: 'The president (who, in accordance with the provisions of Canon B12 "Of the Ministry of the Holy Communion", must have been episcopally ordained priest) presides over the whole service.' The president 'says the opening Greeting, the Collect, the Absolution, the Peace, and the Blessing; [the President] must take the bread and the cup before replacing them on the holy table, say the Eucharistic Prayer, break the consecrated bread, and receive the sacrament on every occasion.' The remaining parts of the service [the president] may delegate to others.[3]

no person shall distribute the elements unless authorised

1.7   As far as distribution is concerned – the sharing of the elements amongst the people – Canon B12:3 states: 'No person shall distribute the holy sacrament of the Lord's Supper to the people unless he shall have been ordained in accordance with the provisions of Canon C1, or is otherwise authorised by Canon, or unless he has been specially authorised to do so by the bishop acting under such regulations as the General Synod may make from time to time.' This has been the consistent Anglican position in ecumenical dialogue.

the bishop is the pre-eminent president of the Eucharist

1.8   The ASB stipulates that 'When necessity dictates, a deacon or lay person may preside over the Ministry of the Word.' It is also said that 'When the Bishop is present, it is appropriate that he should act as president. He may also delegate sections 32–49 [from the Preparation of the Gifts to Communion] to a priest.' This reflects the view that the bishop is the pre-eminent president of the Eucharist.

being a president at the Eucharist means overseeing the celebration

1.9 It is clear, then, that being a president at the Eucharist does not necessarily mean directly leading every part of the service, but it does mean being present as the one who oversees the eucharistic celebration – that is, who has overall responsibility for animating the act of worship as a whole – and, at the very least, who performs the functions described in the ASB rubric just quoted.

'lay presidency': the overseeing of the entire eucharistic celebration by any person who is not an episcopally ordained priest

1.10 The term 'lay presidency' is a slippery one, capable of covering a number of different situations. At one end of the spectrum it might mean permitting a lay person or deacon to preside with, or without, the invitation of the incumbent. At the other end it might refer to a formal authorisation of some sort by the bishop, analogous to the licensing of lay readers. Between these two lie a range of other options. However, the most controversial issue at stake is the theological propriety of a person who is not an episcopally ordained priest 'consecrating and administering' the sacrament.[4] Hence a minimal definition of lay presidency at the Eucharist would be: the consecration and administration of the sacrament by a person who is not an episcopally ordained priest. However, it is generally agreed that the consecration and administration of the sacrament cannot and should not be seen in isolation from the whole eucharistic celebration; in the words of the ASB, the president 'presides over the whole service' even if a part of the service is delegated to others. A more appropriate initial definition of *lay presidency at the Eucharist* would thus be: *the overseeing of the entire eucharistic celebration by any person who is not an episcopally ordained priest*. Unless otherwise stated, this is how 'lay presidency at the Eucharist' will be understood in this statement.

in this context, 'lay' will be taken to include deacons

1.11 Accordingly, we should note that 'lay' and 'laity', when used in the context of eucharistic presidency, are shorthand for 'non-presbyteral', and will be taken to *include* deacons; elsewhere it will be taken to exclude deacons, i.e. to refer to all who are not clergy. This is not to prejudge anything about the ministry of deacons; it is merely to be consistent with the way 'lay' and 'laity' are used in the Synod motion quoted above.

there is a wider sense of 'presidency' – the overseeing of the community in all its worship and mission

1.12 It is worth bearing in mind that there is a wider sense of 'presidency' – the overseeing of the community in all its worship and mission. It will be basic to our argument that these two types of presidency ought to be integrally related. Even so, they remain distinct in meaning, and for the sake of clarity we shall restrict our use of the concept of presidency to the Eucharist. On this see further below, 4.25 and 4.45–6

the interrelation between meanings of the word 'local' needs to be held in mind

1.13   Many of the questions concerning lay presidency are connected with the wish for the Eucharist to be available 'locally'. But the word 'local' as applied to the Church has a variety of meaning. Sometimes this is taken to mean 'in the individual parish, church building or worship centre'.[5] Sometimes it refers to a group of neighbouring parishes associated for the purposes of a local ministry scheme. There is also the classic Anglican understanding that the local Church subsists in the diocese gathered round its bishop. The interrelation between these meanings of the word 'local' needs to be held in mind.

The issue of lay presidency in the Church of England

the history of the Church of England bears out the wording of the motion that lay presidency at the Eucharist is 'incompatible with Anglican tradition'

1.14   The wording of the relevant motion put to General Synod indicates that lay presidency at the Eucharist is 'incompatible with Anglican tradition'. This is clearly borne out throughout the history of the Church of England, and specifically in both the Ordinals and the Act of Uniformity of 1662, the Thirty-nine Articles,[6] the Canons of the Church of England,[7] and, as we have seen, the ASB. With regard to our narrower definition of lay presidency, Canon B12:1 summarises the matter succinctly: 'No person shall consecrate and administer the holy sacrament of the Lord's Supper unless he shall have been ordained priest by episcopal ordination in accordance with the provisions of Canon C1.'[8]

the Book of Common Prayer envisaged no non-ordained Ministry of the Word or the Lord's Supper

1.15   In the Church of England, it is hard to find in the sixteenth and seventeenth centuries any discussion of lay presidency at the Eucharist as we have defined it. The BCP envisaged no non-ordained Ministry of the Word or the Lord's Supper. In the BCP ordination of deacons, the deacon is authorised 'to assist the Priest in Divine Service, and specially when he ministereth the holy Communion, and to help him in the distribution thereof, and to read holy Scriptures and Homilies in the Church ... in the absence of the Priest to baptize infants, and to preach, if he be admitted thereto by the Bishop.' Later the deacon is given authority 'to read the Gospel in the Church of God' (one of his ancient liturgical functions) and to preach, provided he is licensed by the bishop. In the BCP Communion, the deacons, among others, assist at the Offertory. But there is no question of overseeing the Lord's Supper in any sense, and the Act of Uniformity of 1662 makes it clear that only those who have been episcopally ordained priest may 'consecrate and administer the Holy Sacrament of the Lord's Supper'.

the issue was left untouched in the Church of England

1.16   Eucharistic lay presidency was simply not an issue for the English reformers, who restricted presidency to bishops and priests in accordance with the practice of the catholic Church, east and west.[9] Richard Hooker, indeed, precisely in relation to eucharistic ministry argued that 'ministerial power is a mark of separation',[10] and this proved too much for the unknown puritan author of *The Christian Letter*, who specifically asked about the position of lay catechists and readers.[11] As far as we can tell, the issue was still left untouched in the Church of England in the eighteenth century, with a relatively low frequency of celebration and an adequate number of ordained priests. With John Wesley and the growth of the Methodist New Connexion the matter was a live one, though it was only after Wesley's death that non-ordained pastors and ministers administered the sacrament. Within the Church of England, the nineteenth-century Oxford Movement's high view of priesthood grounded in an historical episcopal succession left no room for lay presidency as an acceptable option.

now, a lay person is allowed to officiate at Morning and Evening Prayer, preach, preside over the Ministry of the Word, and assist

1.17   In the middle of the nineteenth century, the office of Lay Reader was inaugurated. This was a revival of the last of the 'minor orders' to survive in the Church of England from the medieval Church. After some debate about reviving Readers in minor orders it was decided to create an office of Reader that was definitely lay, i.e. non-ordained. This acknowledged and eventually promoted the Ministry of the Word by lay people. We are now in a situation when a lay person is allowed to officiate at Morning and Evening Prayer, preach at any service, preside over the Ministry of the Word at a Eucharist in the absence of a priest and assist the president with distribution if authorised to do so. Nevertheless, the impropriety of lay presidency at the Eucharist was largely taken for granted during the period of the English Reformation and subsequently in the Church of England until the 1970s.

attention must be paid to the reasons why the restriction of eucharistic presidency emerged so quickly and became the unbroken practice

1.18   The weight of these historical considerations ought not to be missed. While it is true that 'The doctrine of the Church of England is grounded in the holy Scriptures',[12] and that the Church's faith and practice finds its normative measure in these writings, it is also recognised that the faith of the Church is received and drawn out for each age through traditions which have been tested, cherished, handed on and inhabited through the centuries. It would be foolish to set aside lightly the long, sustained and many-sided tradition which has resisted lay presidency. Careful and generous attention must be paid to the reasons why the restriction of eucharistic presidency to priests/presbyters emerged so quickly and became the unbroken practice of the Church for centuries.

on the other hand, there is no reason to make the matter immune to questioning

1.19   On the other hand, respect for tradition does not entail treating it as a fixed, unalterable deposit. Eucharistic presidency is not a matter addressed directly in Scripture, nor is there any reason to attempt to make it immune to critical theological questioning.

since the 1970s, such questioning has arisen

1.20   Since the 1970s, such questioning has arisen in a number of quarters, especially (but not exclusively) among evangelicals in the Church. Several factors in recent decades have emerged as especially important in making the issue a live one. For example, amongst evangelicals we may note a flourishing interest in the sacraments,[13] resulting from the convergence of a number of streams of thinking and practice – such as the growth of home-groups and the sacramentalism of some currents in the charismatic movement. This has created a desire for communion among some who are generally not as inclined as many in the Church of England to bind together the Eucharist and the ministry of an episcopally ordained priest.

there are also very practical features of Church life which have brought the matter to the fore

1.21   There are also a number of very practical features of Church life which have brought the matter to the fore. Through the influence of the Parish Communion movement, worshippers in many parishes have become used to receiving holy communion on every Sunday. There has been a substantial and relatively steady decline in the number of full-time clergy in the Church of England. In addition, there is the greater longevity of the population which has increased the number of housebound communicants. This has led to situations, especially in rural cures, where a number of parishes or parish centres of worship are under the care of one ordained person who cannot be expected to reach every location every Sunday, thus depriving congregations of the frequency of eucharistic celebration to which they have become accustomed. Related to this, there are times when there are too many sick or housebound people for the ordained minister to bring the sacrament to them as often as he or she would wish.

there has been an increasing number of groups not including a priest

1.22   There has also been an increasing number of groups of Christians who wish to give expression to their fellowship through celebration of the sacrament, groups which will very likely not include an episcopally ordained priest. These may be *ad hoc* groups who come together for a specific purpose, or they may be more consolidated cells or housegroups.

various schemes may be seen to have arisen partly as a response to the same pressures

1.23   Furthermore, there are other practical situations, which, though not new to the Church of England, are sometimes cited as being dealt with most effectively through lay presidency. For example, there may be an interregnum, or the regular priest of the congregation may be ill or away, creating a situation where no readily available ordained substitute can be found. Situations of acute crisis are sometimes also mentioned: when the presiding priest falls ill during a service, or is suddenly called away to deal with some unforeseen difficulty such that there is no time to provide an ordained substitute. Lay presidency is not the only solution offered to these practical problems – among the others have been Extended Communion (see 1.25 below), and various schemes of ordination to local ordained ministry (LOM). Indeed, LOM, including local non-stipendiary ministry (LNSM), and non-stipendiary ministry in general, may be seen to have arisen partly as a considered response to the same pressures as those which have led to a growing interest in lay presidency.[14]

1976: it was said that lay presidency 'would be a real cause for division'

1.24   However, despite renewed interest in lay presidency, relatively little written material on the topic has emerged within the Church of England. The report *The Theology of Ordination*, officially noted by General Synod in 1976, included the first sustained discussion of the issue in an official Church of England document. Against the proposal that the bishop should license a lay person it was said that 'such an action ... would be a real cause for division' within the Church of England.[15] The 'Tiller Report' (1983) proposed that 'in principle' lay leaders should have authority to preside at the Eucharist, and enquires as to 'how one would distinguish theologically between the recognition of that authority and ordination'.[16] A number of individuals from various quarters have advocated schemes of lay presidency. In 1975 A. E. Harvey proposed the occasional celebration by lay people in cases of exceptional need.[17] A case has been outlined by Dr Alan Hargrave, arising out of his experience in the Province of the Southern Cone in South America.[18] Dr David Day[19] and Dr Alwyn Marriage[20] have also advocated a carefully qualified widening of eucharistic presidency beyond the ordained priest.

1993: in the Synod debate on Extended Communion and in subsequent discussion, lay presidency was raised

1.25   In November 1993 the General Synod took note of a report by the House of Bishops on the subject of Extended Communion[21] – that is, the distribution of consecrated elements to communicants on a subsequent occasion in a liturgical setting, generally at some place other than that in which the original eucharistic celebration was held. Draft provision for Extended Communion has been considered by the House of Bishops and the General Synod.[22] In both the Synod debate of 1993 and in the subsequent discussion the matter of lay presidency was frequently raised: the areas of contention with regard to Extended Communion and lay presidency overlap to a considerable extent.

Discussion of lay presidency elsewhere in the Anglican Communion

1988: Lambeth noted the 'received tradition'

1.26   The issue of lay presidency has been before the worldwide Anglican Communion for some time. The Anglican Congress in 1963 made reference to it but the arguments in favour did not gain wide support. Since 1968, the Lambeth Conferences have considered it, though only in passing. In 1984, the Anglican Consultative Council (ACC) favoured 'the ordination of local priests to meet the need' and commended the subject 'for further discussion' at the next meeting of the ACC and Lambeth 1988. The following meeting of the ACC declared that 'the Anglican tradition of priests presiding at the Eucharist should continue to be upheld at this time and that licensing by the bishops of a lay reader for the purpose of ministering the Communion in full should not be encouraged.'[23] The matter was discussed at Lambeth 1988 but the report does not discuss lay presidency *per se*. It speaks of ordaining local people and the use of the reserved sacrament, and notes 'the received tradition that the President at the Eucharist should be a Bishop or Presbyter'.[24]

1995: the International Anglican Liturgical Consultation agreed that separating liturgical function and pastoral oversight tends to reduce liturgical presidency to an isolated ritual function

1.27 In August 1995, the Fifth International Anglican Liturgical Consultation (IALC–5) was convened in Dublin. Nearly 80 Anglican liturgists from 20 provinces and regions of the Communion approved a series of principles and recommendations designed to establish a context for Anglican eucharistic renewal in the coming years.[25] There was extensive treatment of the respective roles of clergy and laity at the Eucharist. Among the principles and recommendations adopted by the whole Consultation were the following:

> In, through, and with Christ, the assembly is the celebrant of the Eucharist. Among other tasks, it is appropriate for lay persons to play their part in proclaiming the word, leading the prayers of the people, and distributing Communion. The liturgical functions of the ordained arise out of pastoral responsibility. Separating liturgical function and pastoral oversight tends to reduce liturgical presidency to an isolated ritual function.'[26]

Accordingly, there is no recommendation of lay presidency – the appropriate group statement, though not approved by the whole Consultation, states that the authorisation of a deacon or lay person to preside at the Eucharist:

> can sever the connection between pastoral and liturgical leadership. If such persons are acting as leaders of a Christian community, they are exercising what are essentially presbyteral functions, and therefore ought to be ordained as presbyters [i.e. priests]. The authorisation by a bishop of a deacon or lay person to preside at the eucharist constitutes an appointment to office, rendering 'lay presidency' a contradiction in terms. Moreover, the sign of appointment to presidential office in Anglican tradition is the laying-on-of-hands and prayer.[27]

Two further significant developments over the last two decades should be mentioned:

the issue has come to the fore in Australia

1.28   Since the 1970s, the issue of lay presidency has come to the fore as a matter of concern within the Anglican Church in Australia, especially in the Diocese of Sydney, leading to a wide-ranging debate.[28] A bill to permit deacons and lay persons to preside at the Eucharist was introduced to the Synod of the Diocese of Sydney in October 1994; its third and final reading has been deferred until July 1997. In March 1996 the Primate referred to the Appellate Tribunal for the opinion as to whether presidency at Holy Communion by a deacon or a lay person was constitutional or not. The Tribunal is expected to give its opinion on this matter in the second half of 1997. In April 1996 the Bishop of Armidale indicated that he had authorised diaconal presidency at Holy Communion in his diocese, as appearing to him to be a better solution than long-term use of reserved sacrament. A working party of the bishops will report on this matter in April 1997. Their discussions have already led to significant moves back from both policies.

in the Southern Cone, a proposal for lay presidency was defeated

1.29   In the geographical area covered by the Province of the Southern Cone in South America, the Anglican Church is tiny, fast-growing, and spread over a vast geographical area with very few ordained ministers. In the 1980s, proposals were discussed in that province and eventually circulated to all other provinces in the Anglican Communion, aimed to provide a flexible pattern of ministry in these very particular circumstances. Among the proposals was that in exceptional circumstances, lay people (including deacons) should be allowed to be licensed by the Bishop to preside at the Eucharist. (A number of specific stipulations were added.) In May 1986, this proposal, in the form of a motion put to the Province of the Southern Cone, was defeated by eight votes to seven.[29]

Dialogue with Churches outside the Anglican Communion

within the Church of England, there is a diversity of opinion on ordination and the theology of the Eucharist

1.30   The Church of England 'professes the faith uniquely revealed in the holy Scriptures and set forth in the catholic creeds ... it has borne witness to Christian truth in its historic formularies, the Thirty-nine Articles of Religion, the Book of Common Prayer, and the Ordering of Bishops, Priests and Deacons'.[30] Within the context of this self-understanding of the Church of England, there is a diversity of opinion on some theological matters, including ordination and the theology of the Eucharist.

account must also be taken of ecumenical debate

1.31   Account must be taken not only of this variety but also of a wider ecumenical debate about the role of ordained and laity at the Eucharist in which the Church of England and other Anglicans have been engaged.

much contemporary Anglican theology has been articulated in an ecumenical context

1.32   Much contemporary Anglican eucharistic theology has been articulated in a self-consciously ecumenical context, and the same applies, of course, to the theology of the roles of clergy and laity at the Eucharist. Much of this ecumenical material is drawn upon in the following pages.

dialogue has been multi-lateral and bilateral

1.33   Dialogue with other Churches has taken place on a multi-lateral and bilateral basis, both nationally and internationally.

in most churches presidency is signified and represented by an ordained minister

1.34   The international multi-lateral text *Baptism, Eucharist and Ministry* (BEM) notes that 'in most churches ... presidency is signified and represented by an ordained minister' (M14), reflecting that although there is little evidence in the New Testament concerning the ordering of the Eucharist, it quickly came about that an ordained ministry presided over the celebration; and reflecting also that this practice is linked to the ministry's functions both of providing a focus for the life and witness of the Church, and also of guiding its apostolic work and witness.

dialogues have implied presidency by presbyters

1.35   International bilateral dialogues with episcopal Churches have usually either affirmed or implied eucharistic presidency by episcopally ordained presbyters.[31]

in the Moravian Church deacons may preside

1.36   In the recently published *Fetter Lane Common Statement*, the report of the Anglican-Moravian Conversations, the text registers agreement that both Churches believe there is a single ordained ministry that takes a threefold form, and that in both Churches only ordained persons are authorised to preside at the Eucharist. In the Moravian Church the probationary status of the diaconate includes authorisation to preside at the Eucharist as well as Confirmation.[32]

in the United Reformed Church lay presidency is allowed in cases of necessity

1.37   The international Anglican-Reformed dialogue *God's Reign and Our Unity* (1984) refers to lay presidency having been a matter of dispute between Anglicans and the Reformed Churches, and notes the Reformed practice of allowing lay presidency in cases of immediate and pressing pastoral necessity, even though the normative pattern should be that the president should be a person who has received the authority to do so through ordination. So, for example, in the current Manual of the United Reformed Church (1995), it is stated that the United Reformed Church shall undertake to 'make provision through district councils, in full consultation with the local Churches concerned, for the recognition of certain members of the United Reformed Church, normally deaconesses, elders or accredited lay preachers, who may be invited by local Churches to preside at baptismal and Communion services where pastoral necessity so requires.'[33]

in the Methodist Church lay presidency may be authorised when needs cannot be met by ordained or probationer ministers

1.38   In the Methodist Church, the matter has received a great deal of attention since the Methodist Union of 1932. In 1946 the Methodist Conference resolved a policy that if a circuit felt that any of its Churches were deprived of reasonably frequent and regular celebration of the sacrament through lack of ordained (presbyteral) ministers, the circuit could apply for the authorisations of persons other than ministers to preside at the Lord's Supper when appointed to do so on the circuit plan, or on other occasions when authorised by the superintendent. Since then, a wide-ranging discussion has ensued. In recent years this has been conducted in the context of a growing awareness and appreciation of the Lord's Supper in the Methodist Church. In 1984, a report on 'lay authorisation' was adopted by the Conference, which, among other things, re-affirmed the principle of 'Extended Communion'. Churches, circuits and districts were invited to discuss the issues raised in the report, sending comments to the Faith and Order Committee by the end of 1995 so that a further report could be brought to the Conference of 1996. That paper proposes that 'deprivation should continue to be the principal ground for authorisation'. A further consideration is in the context of the needs and opportunities for home and hospital communion. Authorisation would only be granted when it was clear that such needs and opportunities could not be met by ordained or probationer ministers.[34]

lay presidency in the Church of England would raise questions where the viability of Anglican orders is already an issue

1.39   The position of Anglicans in dialogue with other Churches, then, has been to affirm the link between episcopally ordained ministry and eucharistic presidency without exception.[35] To allow lay presidency in the Church of England would raise acute questions about future relations with these Churches, especially those (such as the Roman Catholic and Orthodox Churches) whose attitude to the viability of Anglican orders is already very much an issue.[36] While such considerations may not be finally determinative, they must be taken with the utmost seriousness.

Factors involved

roles cannot be discussed without considering critical theological factors

1.40   When considering the respective roles of clergy and laity at the Eucharist, it quickly becomes apparent that this cannot be discussed without considering a significant number of critical theological factors which are implicated on different levels. Further, in addition to this theological context there is also a need to be properly alert to a number of prominent contemporary social attitudes which bear on the matter of eucharistic presidency. In particular, there are those surrounding the notion of representative authority. The responsibility of certain people to act for all is rooted in a sense of relationship between them and the community. The breakdown of that relationship may undermine the authority of the office. We live in a social climate highly sensitive to the abuse of power. We are part of a culture in which anything that can be represented as an exclusive privilege (or peculiar role) is likely to be questioned and challenged. Account will need to be taken of such questionings and suspicions and of the extent to which they can claim specifically Christian, theological support.

beginning with the purposes of God, then ministry, Eucharist and presidency

1.41   Bearing these matters in mind, in what follows we shall begin by considering the place of the worship and mission of the Church within the purposes of the triune God for the world (see Chapter 2). In the light of that we speak of ministry – the ministry of the whole people of God, and within that, the distinctive ministry of the ordained (see Chapter 3). Then we shall turn to the place of the Eucharist in the life of the Church and the role of the eucharistic president (see Chapter 4). In the light of the material covered in Chapters 2 to 4, we shall comment on the principal theological arguments advanced in favour of lay presidency (see Chapter 5) before closing with a summary and conclusions (see Chapter 6).

2

The Church in the purposes of the triune God

theology and an understanding of roles need to be set within the wider context

2.1   A theology of the Eucharist, and an understanding of the respective roles of clergy and laity within it, need to be set within the wider context of a theology of the Church. Approaching the theology of the sacraments and the theology of ordination in this way is rightly assumed in virtually all current writing on ministry and the sacraments, and in all recent major ecumenical documents on these themes.

there has been a shift towards grounding the doctrine of the Church in the Trinity

2.2   Any theology of the Church must ultimately be rooted in the being and acts of God: the Church is first and foremost the people of God, brought into being by God, bound to God, for the glory of God. While this is widely accepted, it has been pointed out that ecclesiology (the doctrine of the Church) in the Church of England (and in many other Churches of the Western tradition) has often paid insufficient attention to the trinitarian character of God, and not least to the distinctive ministry of the Holy Spirit. It is urged that this double neglect has resulted in some damaging consequences for ecclesiology, not least for the way in which ministry and sacraments are understood. Hence, in the last few decades, in the Church of England as in other Churches there has been an undoubted shift towards a more thorough grounding of ecclesiology in the Trinity, together with a fresh interest in the specific action of the Holy Spirit. Among the important contributing factors here have been the growth of the pentecostal and charismatic Churches, the ecumenical movement, post-Vatican II Roman Catholic theology, the growing ministry of women and the house church movement. Crucial also has been a new Anglican engagement with the significant renaissance of trinitarian theology over the last few decades, not least with non-Anglicans who develop ecclesiology from trinitarian roots (e.g. Lossky, Florovsky, Congar, Moltmann and Zizioulas).

this recalls us to aspects which have been sidelined

2.3   There is no claim here that these trends are to be accepted without question, but, arguably, they recall us to aspects of the doctrine of the Church which have too easily been sidelined, and which can greatly enrich a proper appreciation of the respective roles of laity and clergy at the Eucharist. At the very least, they are to be borne in mind as we seek in this chapter to outline an ecclesiology which will best serve our main concerns.

The communion of the Trinity and the communion of the Church

there are different understandings of the Trinity

2.4   The attempt to establish an ecclesiology in immediate relation to God's trinitarian life carries considerable risks. It will be pointed out that there are different understandings of the Trinity, and that the attempt to tie a doctrine of the Church too closely to any particular trinitarian model is more likely to hinder than help us. Some will draw attention to the pliability of trinitarian doctrine for ecclesiology – for example, very different models of ministerial arrangements in the Church have been justified on what is believed to be true of the trinitarian relationships. Some will go further and attack any attempt to trace correlations between the inner life of God and the life of the Church. To speak of God's internal being is at best speculative, at worst arrogant. Also, it is sometimes observed that all Churches will tend to justify their own existing arrangements with the result that trinitarian theology, if deployed, will very likely be distorted to suit political ends. Further, in practice, particular models of the Trinity do not necessarily go hand in hand with corresponding patterns of Church life: as the British Council of Churches Report *The Forgotten Trinity* points out, 'matters of causality in these matters are notoriously difficult to discern.'[1]

nevertheless God has invited us to know him as he is

2.5   Nevertheless, while recognising that it is hazardous to think of any doctrine of the Trinity providing a simple blueprint for ecclesiology, it belongs to the heart of the Christian faith that God, through self-revelation in Christ, has invited us to know him as he eternally is, as irreducibly triune. If the life and action of the Church is grounded in the life and action of this triune God, then our ecclesiology of necessity requires some deliberate attention to trinitarian doctrine.

God's unity is the relation of Father, Son and Spirit

2.6   In the early centuries of the Church the self-revelation of God in Jesus Christ in the power of the Spirit committed the Church to an understanding of God as inherently relational in his being. To speak with John's Gospel of an eternal love between Father and Son 'before the creation of the world' (John 17. 24), to claim with the Council of Nicaea that this Son who became human in Jesus Christ is fully divine – eternally 'one in being' with the Father – is to affirm that relationship belongs to the very being of God. This was developed by the Cappadocian Fathers (late fourth century) who argued that God has his very being in the loving, dynamic communion of Father, Son and Spirit, who mutually indwell one another, exist in one another and for one another, in interdependent giving and receiving. God's unity is the inseparable relation of the particular persons of the Godhead – Father, Son and Spirit.

out of love, God creates and interacts with the world

2.7   The communion of the persons of the Trinity is not to be understood as closed in on itself, but rather open in an outgoing movement of generosity. Creation and redemption are the overflow of God's triune life. Out of that free, unconstrained love which he himself is, God creates the cosmos, a reality other than himself with which he can share his own love, and which will bring him praise. Further, 'From the life of mutuality and fellowship of the Godhead love overflows into creation, sustaining the world in being and bringing it to its appointed glory.'[2] God interacts with the world according to that love at the heart of his being: he relates to his world intensely, drawing all things towards their end, yet in such a way that the world's distinctiveness as created reality is not overridden but enabled to flourish.

God's mission is to reconcile all things to himself

2.8   Human beings are made to live in loving relationship with the triune God and each other, and to articulate and focus the praise of the non-human creation. However, through sin and its effects, the ordered relationships of God's good world have been marred and distorted. Relations between God and humankind, between human persons and between humanity and the non-human world are torn and spoilt (Genesis 1–3). It is the mission of God to restore and renew these broken relationships, to reconcile all things to himself (Colossians 1. 19, 20) through the Son and by the Spirit.

central to this is the bringing into being of a community

2.9   Central to this divine mission lies the bringing into being of a community. Israel is called as the covenant people of God; its members are summoned to live in covenant faithfulness with God and each other, and to gather up and focus the praise of the whole creation. As such Israel is to be a means of blessing to others, a people through whom others might come to live in a fruitful relationship, with God, each other and the created world as a whole. In Jesus Christ, God's purposes for Israel, and for all people through Israel, come to be focused. The eternal Son of God comes as a human being, in whom the sin of his chosen people and of all humanity is reversed and its destructive consequences borne on the cross. In Jesus, humanity has been re-constituted in its proper relationship with the Father. Sinful humanity died on the cross (Romans 8. 3); true humanity, continuous with that sinful humanity but now purged by Jesus' death, rose on Easter morning. Further, the Church is born, called to live out of the re-constituted humanity forged in Jesus Christ.

through the Spirit we are bound to Christ and through him to the Father

2.10   The coming of the eternal Son or Word of God is also the coming of the one through whom all things were created (Colossians 1. 16; Hebrews 1. 2; John 1. 3). In him, through his life, death and rising again, God's damaged creation has been re-ordered towards its end so that it truly praises God. The Spirit is at work in creation (Romans 8), striving to bring about in the world at large what has already been achieved in Christ. Thus, now, through the Spirit, as we are bound to Christ and through him to the Father, we can find our true and intended place in God's world – we can be reconciled to the Father, to each other, and discover our true calling as faithful stewards of the earth. The Church is the community called to embody these felicitous relationships and at the same time to share in God's mission to actualise them in his world.

the Church's members will be drawn together with that love which flows between Father and Son

2.11   Various words have been used to speak of the relation of the Church to the triune being of God. The Church has been described as a 'pattern,' 'icon,' or 'echo' of the Trinity. Whatever language is employed, the concept of participation is crucial. By virtue of the cross and through the Holy Spirit, the Church is given to participate in the eternal filial relationship of love between Son and Father. The Gospels witness to the union between Jesus Christ and his Father (John 10. 30; Matthew 11. 27) and between the Father and the Spirit (John 15. 26), and Jesus prays that his disciples may be drawn into that union (John 17. 21, 22). Therefore, as the Church is caught up in the life of the Spirit, its members will be drawn together with that love which eternally flows between Father and Son (John 17. 21ff.). 'The God whose being is holy love, uniting the Father, Son and Spirit, draws us by the work of the Spirit into participation in the Son's love and obedience to the Father.'[3] The corporate life of the Church is thus 'nothing less than a real participation in the life of the triune God – a life lived always in Christ and offered to the Father through the power of the Spirit.'[4]

the Church is a foretaste of God's kingdom yet is marked by human frailty

2.12   Thus the Church does more than merely point to a reality other than itself. By virtue of its participation in the life of God, it is not only a sign and instrument, but also a genuine foretaste of God's Kingdom, called to show forth visibly, in the midst of history, God's final purposes for humankind. Nevertheless, it also a provisional body, in two main senses. First, only part of the human family has been brought into its life. Second, those who have been brought in are only partly conformed to God's purpose: as a human entity, the Church is marked by all the ambiguity and frailty of the human condition and is constantly in need of repentance, reform and renewal.[5]

in the power of the Spirit, the Church goes with Christ in the mission entrusted to him by the Father

2.13   To share in the triune life of God in this way will entail corporate *worship*, when the Church, sharing in Christ's Communion with the Father through the Spirit, gathers to receive and celebrate its identity, and be built up in its corporate life by hearing the word of God, praying for its own life and the salvation of the world, offering praise and thanksgiving, and enjoying eucharistic fellowship. But to partake of God's life is also to share in his *mission*: the purpose of the Father is to 'reconcile all things to himself, whether on earth or in heaven' in Christ who is both the head of the whole cosmos and head of that body which is sent into the world (Colossians 1. 15–23). It is sent to witness to Christ in word and deed, to call others to know him, to serve all men and women in his name, and to work unceasingly for the establishment of his love and justice. In more fully trinitarian terms, the Church goes with Christ in the power of the Spirit in the mission entrusted to Christ by the Father, to a world of broken relationships. The Holy Spirit, through the faithful words and deeds of the Church, bears witness to Jesus (John 15. 26), brings us to share in the sufferings of Christ (Romans 8. 17) and does his own work of convicting the world (John 16. 8–11) and of leading the Church into a fuller understanding of the Father's will (John 16. 12–15).

the Church is established and sustained through word and sacrament

2.14   In its worship and mission, the Church is established and sustained in the triune God through word and sacrament. The word, the good news culminating in the saving work of God in Jesus Christ and made known supremely through Scripture, is proclaimed, appropriated and followed in the power of the Spirit. The Church is 'grounded in the word of God, preached, believed and obeyed.'[6] Through baptism, by the Spirit, we are incorporated into Christ, made members of his people and acknowledged as children of the Father. Through the Eucharist, the Church is nourished and upheld in its ongoing life, as it is given to share in the Father's gift of the Son through the Spirit.

to speak of the Church as 'communion' carries the meaning of sharing and participation – a dynamic reality

2.15   One way of drawing out further the trinitarian dimensions of the Church's life, which has become commonplace in much ecumenical writing and recent ecclesiology, is to speak of the Church as 'communion' (*koinonia*) – a sharing in the life of the Holy Trinity and therein with fellow-members of the Church.[7] The New Testament word *koinonia* carries the meaning of 'participation' or 'sharing in' which arguably underlies many New Testament descriptions of the Church, though it is worth remembering that the word *koinonia* in the New Testament is always used as an abstract noun (of relationships and activities), not as a concrete noun (a group of people or an institution). *Koinonia* 'implies that the Church is a dynamic reality moving towards its fulfilment.'[8] The uses of *koinonia* with most ecclesiological content are found in 1 John 1. 2, 3 and 1. 6, 7, passages which speak of sharing in the Father and Son, and (deriving from this) the fellowship we have with each other. The phrase '*koinonia* of the Holy Spirit' occurs twice in the New Testament, both in expressions which suggest the Trinity (2 Corinthians 13. 13; Philippians 2. 1): the Spirit generates *koinonia* with God through Christ and with one another.

three points about relationships in the Church

2.16   While keeping in mind the pitfalls of correlating the Church and the Trinity we mentioned above, three relatively uncontroversial points about relationships within the Church may be registered at this stage.

1: there is no difference of worth before God

2: we must begin by thinking of our relatedness to each other – only within this inter-relatedness will the identity of individuals and specific groups properly flourish

3: the Church is a community of persons-in-relation

2.17　　First, just as there is no subordination of being within God – Father, Son and Spirit are co-equally God – so in the communion of the Church, by virtue of our baptism into Christ and thus into the Trinity, there is no difference of value or worth of persons before God (Galatians 3. 28).

2.18　　Second, a trinitarian doctrine of the Church requires us to adopt an essentially relational conception of human personhood, as opposed to one which would picture human beings as basically self-determining individuals. Just as Father, Son and Spirit are what they are because of their intrinsic relationships of giving and receiving with each other, so to be a human person is to be-in-relationship. The Church can never properly be conceived as an assembly of individual believers, nor indeed as an aggregate of essentially independent congregations. To be baptised into the Church is to be baptised into a community of persons who mutually constitute one another through their dynamic relations with each other; individual members discover their identity through their membership of one another. This applies not only to members of a particular worshipping community but to the way in which specific communities make up the universal Church: to belong to a particular community is to belong to the universal, catholic Church. Much damage has been done by doctrines of the Church which begin with the individual, converted believer and then proceed to ask how this believer might be related to others. Similar things could be said of constructing an ecclesiology by speaking of a particular worshipping community and then going on to ask how this group of people might be related to other groups. Undoubtedly the integrity of the individual is of enormous importance in any account of the Church, as is the integrity of a particular worshipping community. But, as the perennial tendency to splintering and denominationalism indicates, we would do better to begin by considering the intrinsic relatedness of all Christians to each other, and then insist that it is only within this inter-relatedness that the identity of individuals and specific groups will properly flourish.

2.19　　Third, we can affirm that as God is what he is by virtue of the dynamic relatedness of Father, Son and Spirit, so the Church is what it is by virtue of the dynamic relatedness of its members. The Church has an institutional dimension to it, and this must not be seen as inherently sinful. However, just as there is no more 'real' God 'behind' Father, Son and Spirit in communion, so the Church is not primarily an institution, existing 'behind' or above its members, but is first and foremost a community of persons-in-relation.

Church and Spirit

these insights are unlikely to gain ground until more attention is paid to the ministry of the Holy Spirit

2.20   It is probable, however, that these insights are unlikely to gain very much ground until, as part of a renewed stress on the trinitarian dimensions of ecclesiology, more attention is paid to the particular ministry of the Holy Spirit. A fairly steady stream of scholarship, claiming widespread support in ecumenical discussions, has suggested that much Western ecclesiology has been characterised by too exclusive a concentration on the second person of the Trinity: Christ inaugurated the Church, the Church comprises those who confess Christ as Lord, and Christ is the ever-present Head and Lord of the Church. The weakness of an over-strong orientation to christology is that it will tend to lay too heavy a stress on the past historical and so institutional aspects of ecclesiology. The Church will come to be seen as possessing an institutional life which it claims it has received from Christ by historical continuity or in some other way, and the Spirit becomes the guarantor of that institution. The Spirit animates a pre-existing institution.[9]

by the Spirit's action the Church is related to Christ, and its members related to each other and to the world

2.21   It needs to be said that neither historical continuity nor the institutional aspect of the Church are to be seen as intrinsically damaging. However, it is arguable that ecclesiology needs to be based as much on pneumatology as on christology. From the beginning, it is by the action of the Spirit that the Church is related to Christ. The Spirit does not simply bring life to an already determined structure, but constantly transforms the community in the present, relating it to Christ, its members to each other and its members to the world in ways which are appropriate to the ever-changing circumstances in which the Church finds itself. The Church ought to be regarded not simply as 'instituted' by Christ but 'constantly *constituted*, i.e. emerging out of the co-incidence and convergence of relationships freely established by the Spirit.'[10] This theme has been a prominent one in pentecostal theology.[11]

Two aspects of the 'constituting' activity of the Spirit in relation to the Church need to be highlighted here.

the Spirit also generates particularity – in the Church, people's distinctiveness is enhanced

2.22   First, there is the Spirit's promotion of distinctiveness and particularity. We have made much of the way in which people are inherently related to one another in the Church, against individualism. However, it needs to be said just as strongly that the Spirit not only binds together but also generates particularity. On the day of Pentecost, the Spirit did not create one uniform language but enabled people to hear each other 'in their own tongues' (Acts 2. 6, 11). It is against uniformity in the Church that Paul protests in 1 Corinthians 12: 'to each the manifestation of the Spirit is given for the common good' (verse 7), and these manifestations are irreducibly different, evidence that 'the body is not made up of one part but of many' (verse 14). Unity in the Spirit does not exist in spite of and in opposition to diversity, but is given with and in it. 'Visible unity ... should not be confused with uniformity.'[12] The Church is a differentiated unity, simultaneously one and many, in which people's otherness and distinctiveness are not effaced but nourished and enhanced in and through their relationships. And this is so because the Church shares in the life of the triune God, who is characterised by the perfect integration of particularity and mutuality, distinctiveness and union.

the Spirit points the Church ahead, to long for the redemption of creation

2.23   Second, there is the Spirit's work of anticipation. In the New Testament, the Holy Spirit is the Spirit of the last days, who brings about in the present the condition of the 'age to come'. Through the Spirit – the 'downpayment' (2 Corinthians 1. 22; Ephesians 1. 14) and 'first-fruits' (Romans 8. 23) of what is to come – the Church already enjoys a foretaste of the end. The Spirit thus points the Church ahead to wait and long in eager expectation for the liberation of the children of God and the redemption of creation (Romans 8. 18–25). The Church cannot forget that she lives in the overlap between the 'old' and 'new age'. She is confident, by sharing through the Spirit in Christ, of an authentic sharing in the reality of the final fulfilment, but also acutely aware that it has not yet arrived and that humankind and creation are only partly conformed to God's purpose.

One, holy, catholic and apostolic

'sharing in the communion of God' and the four marks of the Church:

2.24   To conclude this chapter, and to prepare the way for the following chapters, we should note that the pattern of relationships engendered by the Church's sharing in the triune communion of God can be linked to what have traditionally been known as the four 'marks of the Church', enunciated in the Nicene Creed – oneness, holiness, catholicity and apostolicity.[13]

1: the one Church is called to share in God's oneness of persons-in-relation

2.25   The Church is *one* in that, through sharing by the Spirit in the new redeemed humanity of Christ and in his communion with the Father, it has been given to participate in, and is called to grow deeper into that unity which characterises the triune God. As we have seen, a trinitarian theology of the Church will speak of the oneness of the Church not as a homogenous unity, but as a differentiated oneness of distinctive persons-in-relation who discover their particularity in active relationships of giving and receiving.

2: the holy Church is summoned to a life of loyalty to the triune God

2.26   The Church is *holy* in that it has been claimed by, and is summoned to a life of dedicated loyalty to the triune God of Jesus Christ. This is only possible because of Christ's holiness – in order that we might become holy, he has sanctified himself by obedience to the Father to the point of death on the cross (John 17. 19). Through the Spirit, we are given to participate in the holiness of

Christ and his Father, living in God's world as God's ethically distinct people, embodying and promoting just relationships in a world of distorted and fragmented relationships.

3: the catholic Church is a community reaching out to embrace all

2.27   The Church is *catholic* both because Christ is there, and also because it is sent to all the world. The Church shares in the communion of Father, Son and Spirit who are intrinsically related in communion and whose communion opens out to the world in sheer, unmerited grace. Thus its members are intrinsically related to each other as constituent members of one vast community, a community which reaches out to embrace every generation, race, colour, gender or class.

4: the apostolic Church is sent by Christ as he is sent by the Father, carried forward in its mission by the Spirit

2.28   The Church is *apostolic* in that it is grounded in, and summoned to be true to, the apostolic faith. It is also apostolic in that it is 'sent' ('apostled') in every generation: as Christ is sent by the Father, so the Church is sent by Christ. These two aspects of apostolicity are inseparable: faithfulness to apostolic teaching means the Church can never forget its missionary calling, and authentic mission must be true to the apostolic faith. Here, once again, it is important that a fully trinitarian understanding of apostolicity is achieved, giving due attention to the specific work of the Spirit. There have been times when apostolicity and 'apostolic succession' have been conceived almost exclusively in historical and christological terms, as a backward orientation through history to the career of Jesus and the apostolic Church. The danger is that the Church's mission will become little more than an attempt to preserve, re-live, or replicate an ancient tradition in the present. Irreplaceable as the foundational history of Jesus is, we are related not simply historically through time to a 'past Christ' but by means of the Spirit to the living Christ now, in whose continuing ministry we participate. The Spirit enables fidelity to and continuity with apostolic faith but constantly actualises and particularises this tradition afresh in the present, so that the truth of Christ is brought alive for the ever new situations with which the Church engages in its missionary calling. This is integral to the Spirit's eschatological ministry[14] – to carry the Church forward in its mission, anticipating here and now in ever fresh ways the Father's final, eschatological desire.

3

The Church's ministry and ministries

implications of the nature of the Church for understanding its ministry

3.1   In the last chapter, we considered some points concerning the nature of the Church. We shall now explore their implications for the way we understand ministry within the Church, giving special attention to the relation between clergy and laity. This will provide the context in which we shall set our discussion of the Eucharist in the next chapter.

General comments

there is no difference of persons' value before God

3.2   We have said that just as there is no subordination of being within the triune God, nor, by extension, can there be difference of value of persons before God within the communion of the Church by virtue of our baptism in the triune name (2.17). Nevertheless, two general comments by way of qualification need to be made.

but there is a diversity of responsibilities and relationships

3.3   First, it is generally accepted that although there is no subordination of being, there is nevertheless differentiation of function and relationship within the Trinity. For example, it is the Son who lives in obedience to the Father and not vice versa; the Father relates to both Son and Spirit, but in different ways. So, too, there can and should be a diversity of responsibilities and relationships within the Church – a theme classically expounded by Paul in 1 Corinthians 12.

patterns of order between the persons of the Trinity exist without superiority of personhood

3.4   Second, something needs to be said about order in the Church in relation to the Trinity. Much debate surrounds this area. For example, it is generally agreed that in a number of places the New Testament affirms (or implies) a certain 'priority' of the Father in both the acts and the being of God. The word 'God' by itself often means 'God the Father'. The Father initiates the work of creation and to him everything is directed (1 Corinthians 15. 24ff.); it is the Father '*from* whom all things came and for whom we live' and the Son '*through* whom all things came and through whom we live' (1 Corinthians 8. 6). Although there is disagreement as to exactly what this might mean for the patterning of relationships within the Church, nevertheless we can surely say that patterns of order and responsibility between the persons of the Trinity exist without any inferiority or superiority of personhood, dignity or being. The humiliation of Jesus is, after all, a mark of his divinity and glory, not his inferiority.

relationships within the Trinity are fully mutual and reciprocal

3.5   In this connection, it is important to see that relationships within the Trinity are fully mutual and reciprocal: they are constituted by mutual interaction, giving and receiving. The obedience of Jesus to the Father is a freely given commitment, not resigned submission or servility to a greater power. The Father's identity and role in the trinitarian life is dependent upon loving and free acceptance on the part of the Son and the Spirit. Likewise, within the Church, while there can be no difference of worth of persons in the sight of God, relationships of obedience and accountability between members may properly exist; and, provided they are practised within free relationships of mutual giving and receiving, they are able to promote the fulfilment of the Church's calling.

The ministry of the people of God: sharing in the priesthood of Christ

all Christian ministry derives from Christ's, and through baptism all are called to ministry and service

3.6   With these points in mind, we can now consider more fully ministry and ministries within the Church. First and foremost we must maintain that 'The primary ministry is that of the risen Christ himself, and we are enabled to participate in it by the power of the Spirit.'[1] All Christian ministry derives from and shares in Christ's ministry. There can be no Christian ministry apart from Christ, for his self-offering and self-emptying alone reconciles the world to the Father and people to each other. Through baptism, all Christians are called to a ministry and service as God's fellow-workers: 'baptism ... projects us into the ministry of reconciliation'.[2]

Christ the High Priest offered himself and lives to intercede for us

3.7   The theme of Christ's ministry is developed in the Epistle to the Hebrews in terms of Christ as our High Priest. The Son who is the 'radiance' of God (1. 3) comes as one of us, and in solidarity with us makes the perfect, obedient self-offering to God, culminating in his offering made on the cross through the eternal Spirit (9. 14). The priest who once offered himself now acts as our permanent High Priest (7. 24), living to intercede for us (7. 24, 25; cf. Romans 8. 34). Through him we find forgiveness and enter confidently into the holy presence of God (10. 19).

the Church is described collectively as a priesthood

3.8   The Church now shares in the priesthood of Christ. Though this theme is not developed at length in the New Testament, the Church is described collectively as a priesthood: 'you are a chosen race, a royal priesthood, a holy nation, God's own people, that you may declare the wonderful deeds of him who called you out of darkness into his marvellous light' (1 Peter 2. 9). The priestly function of the people in 1 Peter is described as declaring God's praises (2. 9), and offering 'spiritual sacrifices' (2. 5). This corporate priesthood is dependent upon and derived from the priesthood of Christ, in the double sense that it is only possible because of what has been accomplished once for all (compare Revelation 1. 5, 6, where we are told that it is through Christ's blood that he has 'made us a kingdom, priests to serve his God and Father', and Revelation 5. 9, 10 for the same idea), and that the 'spiritual sacrifices' the Church now offers can only be made acceptable through Christ (1 Peter 2. 5).

as a body, it shares in the unique priesthood of Christ

3.9   Thus the entire Church, corporately, in its worship and mission participates in the continuing priesthood of Christ. Through union with Christ, the members of his body have access to the Father in the Spirit and are enabled to make an offering which is truly their own, yet only in, and with, and through, and wholly dependent on the offering of Christ. In Reformation thought, this was articulated in the concept of the 'priesthood of all believers', which has been described as a 'paraphrase of the Reformation concept of the Church'.[3] It is an Old Testament notion transferred from Israel in Exodus 19. 6 to the Church in 1 Peter 2. 9. When properly expounded in relation to 1 Peter and Hebrews, it does not, as is often thought, refer primarily to the ministry of individuals, but to the fact that the Church as a body shares in the unique priesthood of Christ and thus has access to the Father.[4]

The ministries of the people of God

diverse roles are essential to the Church's well-being: they are to be practised within relationships of mutual giving and receiving – but there is a danger of ministries being oriented purely towards the Church's inner life

3.10   Nevertheless, the Church's corporate priesthood does not iron out diversity. As we have said above, diverse roles are essential to the Church's well-being. Different ministries are given by the ascended Christ (as in Ephesians 4. 12b–16), and realised through the Spirit amongst the Church (1 Corinthians 12. 7ff.). Two points in particular ought to be stressed concerning these ministries. First, though distinct, they cannot be seen in isolation from each other, for they are to be practised within relationships of mutual giving and receiving, in such a way that the whole body of the Church is built up (1 Corinthians 12). Second, as the Church of England Report *All are Called* highlighted, there is a very real danger that the ministries of the people of God will be understood as oriented purely towards the inner life of the Church.[5] For the majority of Christians, their ministry is exercised in living the Christian life in their family and in their job, and in witnessing by the character of their life and their work, and by speech when occasion offers.[6] For some Christians it will mean exercising particular gifts, such as healing, teaching, prophecy, social care and evangelism. For some it may be in whole or in part in some particular office for which they have been trained and commissioned by the Church, such as Readers, evangelists, pastoral assistants. For some it may be a vocation to serve in a religious community under rule and vows. Whatever it is, it will be focused in and derived from their regular worship as Church members.[7]

Emergent patterns of ministerial leadership

community leadership appears to have been basic to the first Christian congregations

3.11   In addition to these ministries just mentioned, there is what is sometimes referred to as the 'distinctive ministry'. We have said above that 'ordering' of ministries need not be regarded as inherently suspect or problematic. From the very beginning in the Church there were various arrangements of responsibilities such that there was both recognised authority and accountability. Community leadership in various forms appears to have been basic to the first Christian congregations, with no indication that this was some kind of necessary evil, or implied any intrinsic superiority of these leaders over other Christians. Thus, for example, the writer of 1 Peter seems quite content to assume *both* the priestly ministry of the whole people (2. 4–10) and the oversight of particular people, an oversight desired by God (5. 1–5, where the ministry of oversight is explicitly described as a pastoral ministry, patterned on the model of Christ the Good Shepherd: cf. also John 21. 15–17).

the ministry of leadership is a gift of God – it is a ministry of authority, but, as with all ministry, it is a ministry of service

3.12   As is well known, it is notoriously dangerous to use the New Testament to sanction particular types of community leadership today. 'All attempts to read off one divinely authorised form of [ordained] ministry from the New Testament are futile.'[8] It is clear that the ministry of leadership is not regarded as a human invention but a gift of God to his Church. It is a ministry of authority, but, as with all ministry, it is a ministry of service, following Christ's precept (Mark 10. 42–45) and example (John 13. 4ff.). In addition, the apostles appear to have exercised a ministry of fundamental significance. They were characterised by a special relationship with the historical Christ, a commission from him to the Church and the world, and the gift of the Spirit at Pentecost, undertaking oversight and pastoral care through visits and by letter, and, it would seem, holding different congregations together in unity. As far as community leaders are concerned, the early New Testament documents do not provide precisely defined ministerial functions and actions, though explicit 'emphasis is given to the proclamation of the word and the preservation of apostolic doctrine, the care of the flock and the example of Christian living.'[9] There are strong indications that local Christian communities were kept in touch with each other through those who, like Paul, were founders of the communities, and through something akin to synodical oversight (cf. e.g. Acts 15).

the beginnings of 'ordination' can be discerned

3.13   The first Churches probably displayed a considerable variety of structure in their pastoral ministry. It is clear that some (though probably not all) were headed by ministers who were called *episcopoi* (bishops/overseers) and *presbuteroi* (presbyters). These terms could be applied to the same man or to men with identical or very similar functions, and a single Church might include more than one *episcopos* (see e.g. Titus 1. 7 in the context of the preceding verses). 'The evidence suggests that with the growth of the Church the importance of certain functions led to their being located in specific officers of the community.'[10] Further, some form of recognition and authorisation appears to have been required in the New Testament period for those who exercise the functions of leadership. The beginnings of what was later to be called 'ordination' as a formal rite can be discerned, with the laying on of hands (associated with the operation of the Spirit: cf. e.g. Acts 13. 2, 3). In the Pastoral Epistles, this commissioning for service may mean recognition of an existing ministry exercised in the Spirit (1 Timothy 4. 14) or 'appointment' to such a ministry (2 Timothy 1. 6). In these letters we also see the emergence of presbyters exercising *episcope* or pastoral oversight as first among equals, whose main task was to safeguard faithfulness to the apostolic teaching.

a threefold ministry of bishops, presbyters and deacons appears, though with variation from place to place

3.14   By the time of Ignatius (c. 110 AD), a threefold pattern of ministry – a bishop sharing his ministry of oversight of a particular community, assisted by presbyters (a kind of governing council) and deacons (most likely, a kind of personal assistant to the bishop) – seems to have taken hold in Syria and Asia Minor and is soon found more generally, though we must bear in mind that there would have been considerable variation of practice from place to place. These were ministries of the local worshipping congregation, the bishop being the principal link in faith, mission and unity between his and other congregations. In time the bishop became the leader of several congregations, i.e. his office became a regional one, while the presbyters became the shepherds of these congregations.[11]

the Church grew in complexity – with ambiguities and dangers

3.15   The ordinary processes of institution-building are evident in these and later developments. They were bound to occur as the Church grew in size and complexity, and there were costs attached to them. Our view of them may be that they took place under the promised guidance of the Holy Spirit, but were not free of ambiguities and dangers. From the very first it was anticipated that the exercise of the responsibilities of leadership in the Church entailed the risk of domineering behaviour (Luke 22. 24–27; 1 Peter 5. 1–4).

all ministry must have a personal, collegial and communal character

3.16   A basic pattern of a pastor, a collegial association for the pastor, and pastoral assistants to carry out ministry in the world is one that has been adopted by the large majority of Churches in one form or another to the present day. In recent ecumenical discussion this has been expressed in terms of three dimensions of ministry: the personal, collegial and communal (synodical), exercised at the local, regional and universal levels of the Church's life.

As God in Christ deals with us in a personal [i.e. individual] way, so all ministry must have a *personal* character, providing in a specific person a focus for the unity and witness of the community. As God calls us into a reconciled fellowship, so all ministry must have a *collegial* character – exercised not by one person alone but in shared responsibility with colleagues. As the Church is the body of Christ quickened by the Spirit, so the ministry must have a *communal* character, so that every member is enabled to exercise the gifts which the Spirit gives and so that the whole community is, as far as possible, associated in the process of teaching and decision making.

(God's Reign and Our Unity (1984), par. 92)

there has been agreement that oversight is necessary

3.17   There has been considerable agreement in contemporary ecumenical dialogue that 'a ministry of pastoral oversight (*episcope*), undertaken in personal, collegial and communal ways, is necessary as witness to and safeguard of the unity and apostolicity of the Church'.[12]

the Anglican Communion maintains the three-fold order

3.18   In the Anglican Communion the three-fold order of bishop, priest/presbyter and deacon has become established.[13] In maintaining this order, the Anglican Church stands with other episcopal Churches. In most protestant Churches who hold to this pattern, the main functions of the threefold ministry are exercised by the members of a single ministry acting in certain matters individually and in others collectively.

but it is not clear that it has always struck a balance between the three ministerial dimensions

3.19   However, it is not clear that the threefold Anglican ordained ministry has always been practised in such a way that an appropriate balance has been struck between the three ministerial dimensions outlined in 3.16. The Reformed Churches, for instance, have expressed concern that in the Anglican tradition the personal dimension may become so dominant at times that it is isolated from the community and no longer exercised in relation to the responsibility of the synod.[14]

Lay and ordained

at various stages, the Church of England has fallen prey to the process of clericalisation – where clergy come to be regarded as separate from, and superior to the laity

3.20   There is little doubt that a satisfactory understanding of the relation between the ordained ministry and the ministry of the whole people of God has been hampered by a complex process usually called 'clericalisation' – where clergy come to be regarded as essentially separate from, and superior to the laity. The common use of the word 'laity' to mean 'non-ordained' itself testifies to this. In the last chapter we noted tendencies in the West to over-stress the Church's 'institution' by Christ to the detriment of its 'constitution' by the Spirit. This has often led to a view of ordination which overplays the minister's historical continuity with Christ and loses sight of the intrinsic relation between ordained ministry and the life of the whole Church, a life which is constantly being re-constituted in its multiplicity of ministries by the Spirit. Thus Edward Schillebeeckx points to what he calls a 'pneumatological and ecclesial' understanding of the Church's ministry in the first millennium of its history over against a 'direct Christological' one in the second millennium. He argues that whereas previously the ministry of the Church emerged *from* within the community *for* the leadership of the community and was, therefore, the product of the Spirit-filled character of the people, latterly the ministry became theoretically and practically detached from the community and came to be seen as the product of a direct historical link with Christ through the 'apostolic succession.'[15] As is well known, by the late medieval period we witness an intensification of these tendencies which served to drive a deep wedge between clergy and laity. Exaggerated claims were made for the institutional aspects of the Church and for the office and function of the ordained ministry, with damaging consequences for the relationship between laity and clergy. At various stages in its history, the Church of England has itself fallen prey to this process of clericalisation, and at times has been hindered by narrowly christological theologies of ordination.[16]

recently we find an insistence that ordination takes no one 'out' of the laity

3.21   In view of this, we find in much recent Anglican ecclesiology and ecumenical agreement, not only a distinct accent on the present ministry of the Spirit (to which we shall return), but also a repeated insistence that ordination takes no one 'out' of the laity. The ordained ministry is inherently related to the ministry of the whole body and must never be regarded as separable from it. In the last chapter (2.19) we criticised the tendency to treat the institutional aspect of the Church as somehow more authentic than the people who make up the Church; likewise, any proclivity to consider ordained ministers – insofar as they are part of the institutional government of the Church – as more authentic or 'real' than the non-ordained needs to be strenuously resisted.

it has proved anything but easy to articulate satisfactorily the relationship between ordained and non-ordained – 'focus' can be a positive or negative metaphor

3.22   It is also a recurrent theme of Anglican and ecumenical ecclesiology that the ordained ministry is provided to strengthen and build up the royal priesthood of the Church: in the words of the Porvoo Statement, ordained ministry 'exists to serve the ministry of the whole people of God.'[17] However, it has proved anything but easy to articulate satisfactorily the relationship between ordained and non-ordained in such a way that the ministry of the whole people of God is seen as neither inferior to, nor superior to, nor in competition with the ministry of the clergy.[18] A metaphor which has gained some currency in recent discussion is that of 'focus'.[19] This can be used in a positive sense, in that the ordained are to draw out the potential inherent in the Church as a whole, in a way that fosters and evokes the growth of the potential of others without seeking to control the outcome of growth. But, negatively, the metaphor could accommodate the mistaken view that the ordained subsume into their own ministry all that belongs to lay people, as if all the gifts seen in a congregation are found in a sharper way in the clergy and all ministry relates to the presence and action of the ordained. On this view, the clergy would have the same kind of responsibilities and ministry as lay people but in a more concentrated form. By the same token, lay ministry would be seen as a diluted form of ordained ministry.

likening the distinctiveness of the ordained to the dignity and role of the Father within the triune God carries dangers

3.23   The distinctiveness of the ordained has sometimes been likened to the dignity and role of the Father within the triune God. In traditions which have come to stress the priority of the Father within the Trinity – as the 'origin' of Son and Spirit – it is sometimes said that ultimate authority resides in the Father, the Son ministers the Father's will and possesses delegated authority of his own, and the Spirit serves the authority of Father and Son. Such models, however, carry dangers, not just in themselves but also when applied directly to the ordained/lay relation. First, the ordained leader or leaders are not the 'source' of the Church in a way parallel to the Father within the Godhead. Second, this kind of model can suggest a picture of lay people as there simply to be led by clergy, as objects of teaching and administrative clerical authority. It is worth recalling that the Father's identity and role in the Trinity are dependent on the free and loving acceptance of the Son and Spirit (3.3). The ordained leader of a community may represent the whole Church in a public and acknowledged way, but they represent others only insofar as others recognise, allow and confirm this. Third, the model can also too easily imply that the non-ordained only have authority when it is delegated to them from the clergy.

objections to metaphors of 'derivation' and 'enhancement' are similar to those directed against the use of the word 'focus'

3.24   Metaphors of 'derivation' and 'enhancement' have also been employed: the ordained ministry is derived from, or enhances the ministry of the non-ordained. The objections to this are similar to those directed against the use of the word 'focus'. The ordained ministry will inevitably be regarded as a 'magnified' or concentrated version of the common ministry, sharing in Christ's ministry to a 'greater degree' than the non-ordained. The point was made in the report entitled *The Priesthood of the Ordained Ministry* presented by the Faith and Order Advisory Group of General Synod in 1986:

> The special ministry is ordained to speak and act in the name of the whole community. It is also ordained to speak and act in the name of Christ in relation to the community. Its authority and function are therefore not to be understood as simply delegated to it by the community. Consequently, in so far as its ministry is priestly, its priesthood is not simply derived from the priestliness of the whole community. Rather the

common priesthood of the community and the special priesthood of the ordained ministry are both derived from the priesthood of Christ. Bishops and presbyters do not participate to a greater degree in the priesthood of Christ; they participate in a different way – not that is as individual believers, but in the exercise of their office. Thus theirs is not a magnified form of the common priesthood; the difference is this, that their ministry is an appointed means through which Christ makes his priesthood present and effective to his people.

(*The Priesthood of the Ordained Ministry* (1986), par. 42.)

'priests' exercise their priestly ministry by virtue of their participation, with the whole body, in Christ's priestly ministry

3.25   More succinctly, the Anglican-Reformed Report, *God's Reign and Our Unity* states that:

'Priests' exercise their priestly ministry neither apart from the priesthood of the whole body, nor by derivation from the priesthood of the whole body, but by virtue of their participation, in company with the whole body, in the priestly ministry of the risen Christ, and as leaders, examples and enablers for the priestly ministry of the whole body in virtue of the special calling and equipment given them in ordination.

(par. 80)

Ordination and the four marks of the Church

the ordained ministry is a gift of God to promote, release and clarify all other ministries

3.26   We would suggest that, in relation to the people of God as a whole, *the ordained ministry is best conceived as a gift of God to his Church[20] to promote, release and clarify all other ministries in such a way that they can exemplify and sustain the four 'marks' of the Church – its oneness, holiness, catholicity and apostolicity.* The ordained ministry is a sign of, and a means of drawing out the four marks of the Church, helping to bring about and realise in others the different ways in which the Church can participate in the priesthood of Christ and thus in the purposes of the triune God.[21]

the priest/presbyter and bishop have primary responsibility for the leadership and formation of the community according to its four marks

3.27   In the Church of England, the priest/presbyter and bishop have primary responsibility for the leadership and formation of the community according to its four marks. This is a ministry of word and sacrament. The word, the good news climaxing in Jesus Christ and made known supremely through Scripture, is learned, lived, preached and pronounced to penitent sinners in forgiveness and absolution. It is applied in pastoral care, intercession, encouragement and discipline. The word is signed and sealed through the administration of the sacraments of baptism and the Eucharist.

as Christ distributes ministries through the Spirit, priests share in Christ's distribution of these gifts

3.28   As ministers of word and sacrament, the ordained act 'in the name of Christ'. Article XXVI of the Thirty-nine Articles speaks of ministers of word and sacrament 'not [ministering] in their own name, but in Christ's and . . . by his commission and authority'.[22] This is not to exclude the participation of others in Christ's ministry, nor to suggest that such participation can take place only through the ordained priest. Rather, the Church as a whole participates in the priesthood of Christ, and as Christ distributes ministries through the Spirit, priests share in Christ's distribution of these gifts – without being the sole or primary imitators of Christ – so that the whole Church is established in its four marks.

at ordination a minister is set in a distinctive and permanent relationship to the Church as a whole

3.29   Those who are ordained do not stand apart from the Church community; rather, those who are to be ordained are called from within the community, and are then returned to serve within that community, though standing in a new relationship to it. This is not to be understood simply in terms of the community of a particular locality. From the earliest days of the Church, it appears that ministerial oversight both served particular worshipping congregations and held a number of congregations together in a wider communion of faith, a communion which ultimately embraced all baptised members of the Church. At ordination a minister is set in a distinctive relationship to the Church as a whole, and this is a permanent relationship, signified by the use of the traditional term *character*.[23] He or she will also be licensed to exercise his or her ministry in a particular locality and within certain limits, thus giving expression in the local community to this ministerial relationship to the whole Church, but though this licensing is included in ordination, it is not itself ordination.

ordination, though an act of the triune God, must also be seen as an act of the Church

3.30   In line with this, ordination, though an act of the triune God, must also be seen as an act of the Church. As we have said above, the ordained can properly represent others only insofar as others recognise, allow and confirm this ministry. The Church, local and universal, elicits, tests and ratifies the ordinand's calling, and seeks to foster his or her particular gifts through careful preparation. When he or she is ordained to a particular work by the bishop, the appropriate local Christian community recognises and receives the person in that capacity. And the universal Church, in the person of the bishop, acknowledges that God gives to this person this particular gift of service to be used for the good of his people.

ordination and the four marks of the Church:

3.31   To draw out further the characteristics of the ministry of a priest/presbyter and bishop, we can relate ordination to each of the four marks of the Church in turn, of which we have already spoken (2.24–2.28).

I: the ordained minister carries a responsibility to foster unity-in-diversity and to be a focus of unity

3.32   The Church is *one* in that it has been given to share in, and is called to grow deeper into the unity of the triune God (see 2.25). The ordained minister as leader carries a specific responsibility to foster the unity-in-diversity which we believe God seeks to bring about in his Church for the sake of the world. In addition, the ordained leader is to be a focus of unity for the particular congrega-tion(s) for which he or she is responsible. The leader not only speaks and acts in the name of Christ, but also for the community in its plurality, as 'one on behalf of the many'. The Church is represented in that person as he or she carries the concerns of the flock. The ordained person can be both a means of renewing unity and a sign of it.[24]

2: to promote the holiness of the Church and to be a 'whole-some example'

3.33   The Church is *holy* in that it is claimed by, and summoned to a life of fidelity to the holy, triune God (2.26). The ordained leader carries a specific responsibility to promote the holiness of the Church in all aspects of its worship and mission, by pointing to, and enabling the Church to share in the holiness of God. Further, while the holiness of the Church must never be entirely dependent on the holiness of its ordained ministers, it is clearly a responsibility of the ordained to be 'a wholesome example of (and to) the flock of Christ'.[25] The minister is to foster habits of lifestyle, prayer, penitence, self-criticism and self-awareness which will open up ways for others to share more fully in God's holiness. Thus the ordained can be both a means of renewing holiness and a sign of it.

3: to act representa-tively not only for a particular community but for the Church universal – a sign of the catholicity of the Church as well as a means of renewing it

3.34   The Church is *catholic* in that its members are inherently related to each other as members of a community which reaches out to all people (2.27). We have already touched on the catholicity of ordination above (3.29–3.30). Ordination relates not only to the community or communities of a particular locality but to the one universal Church. The ordained are part of networks within which the wholeness and inter-relatedness of the catholic Church as a reflection of the Trinity can be achieved and made visible. At an ordination, invocation is made to the Father in the name of Christ to grant his Spirit to the one ordained to the office and work to which that person is called, with the intent that the ordination car-ries the authority to act representatively not only for a particular community or communities but for the Church universal in the ways proper to that particular office. Thus God's call to ordination is testified and corroborated not only by the local congregation(s) but by the whole Church in the person of the bishop: those to be ordained are to be received by the Christian community of a local-ity but also by the bishop acting in the name of the universal Church. The ordained ministry can be a means whereby the local Church is represented to the universal Church and the universal to the local. The local is set in the wider context of the universal Church and the life of the universal Church brought to bear in the local setting.[26] The ordained can thus be both a sign of the catholicity of the Church through episcopal ordination, as well as a means of renewing it.

4: 'apostolic succession' is the succession of the whole Church in the apostolic faith

3.35　　The Church is *apostolic* in that it is rooted in and called to be true to the apostolic faith (2.28). Hence apostolicity should not be restricted to the ordained: 'The witness to the gospel has been entrusted to the Church as a whole. The whole Church as the *ecclesia apostolica* stands in the apostolic succession.'[27] 'Apostolic succession' is first and foremost the succession of the whole Church in the apostolic faith. It is an expression of the permanence and, therefore, of the continuity of Christ's own teaching and mission in which the Church participates.

the historical succession of ordained ministry, expressed particularly in the episcopal succession, serves this continuity

3.36　　The historical succession of ordained ministry serves this continuity, and in the Anglican Communion, as in many others, this continuity finds particular expression in the episcopal succession. In line with much contemporary ecumenical understanding we believe that the historic episcopate is a sign of, and serves, the apostolicity of the whole Church, constituting a call to fidelity and to unity, a summons to witness to, and a commission to realise more fully 'the permanent characteristics of the Church of the apostles.'[28] The laying on of hands by bishops who have had hands laid on them in succession signifies continuity back to the Apostles.[29] However, the historic episcopate does not guarantee the fidelity of the Church to every aspect of the apostolic faith (nor the individual faithfulness of the bishop). Indeed, it must be acknowledged that such apostolic faithfulness has been preserved in Churches which have not retained the sign of the historic episcopate.[30]

the ordained have a particular responsibility to ensure that the Church is true to its missionary calling

3.37　　The Church is also apostolic in that it is 'sent' ('apostled') in every generation. As Christ is sent by the Father, so the Church is sent by Christ. This sending belongs to the whole Church; all members are called to share in the Church's apostolic mission. In relation to the missionary calling of the whole people of God, the ordained have a particular responsibility to ensure that the Church is true to its missionary calling in, to and for the sake of the world. The priest is called to re-call the people of God to their apostolic vocation, and therefore stands over against the community as well as being part of it.

the ordained ministry is apostolic – not simply holding the Church faithful to a particular past, but enabling it to actualise the faith in ways apt for today

3.38　　We noted earlier that these two aspects of apostolicity need to be related with special attention to the Ministry of the Holy Spirit (2.28). The Spirit enables continuity with apostolic faith but also ceaselessly particularises the faith in the present, so that the truth of the Gospel is brought alive for the ever new contexts which the Church faces as she is drawn towards the future pledged in Jesus Christ. Seen from this perspective, the ordained ministry is apostolic in that it is a means not simply of holding the Church faithful to a particular past, but of enabling the Church to actualise the apostolic faith in ways which are fitting and apt for the circumstances of today in anticipation of God's promised future.

4

The Eucharist, the Church and eucharistic presidency

we now set the Eucharist in the context of the ministry of the whole people of God

4.1   In the last chapter we offered an account of the ministry of word and sacrament in relation to the ministry of the whole people of God. It is now our task to set the Eucharist in this context, bearing in mind that the General Synod has requested 'a statement about the theology of the Eucharist'. Clearly, the vast amount of literature which has and still appears on the Eucharist rules out even the attempt at an outline of a comprehensive theology of the Eucharist, let alone a statement which will deal at any depth with all the prominent matters of controversy. The Synod motion makes it clear that particular attention is to be paid to the roles of clergy and laity at the Eucharist, and it is with this in mind that we proceed.

Trinitarian feast[1]

the Eucharist is a means of a genuine sharing in Christ – it does not simply help the participant to meditate on the saving significance of the cross; it mediates the gift of Christ's saving presence

4.2   To begin with, we affirm that the Eucharist is a means of a genuine sharing in Christ, of an authentic union with him. Here Christ renews his engagement with those he has claimed through baptism. This is expressed at the Last Supper in the giving of the bread and the cup: both effect a bond with Christ. It underlies the eucharistic theology of both Paul and John in the New Testament – for them, it is axiomatic that the Gospel involves a sharing in Christ himself, in his life, death and resurrection, and it is against that horizon that they set the Eucharist (1 Corinthians 10. 14–22, 11. 17–34; John 6. 25–58). This sharing is neither magical nor automatic: it is to be discerned and recognised (an important stress in Paul) and is bound up with the faith which is the gift of God (especially important for John). The Eucharist does not simply help the participant to meditate on the saving significance of the cross; it mediates the gift of Christ's saving presence. This was also fundamental for many of the mainline reformers, including Cranmer.

in the Eucharist Christ's sacrifice is celebrated and proclaimed

4.3   The Eucharist is a means of sharing in the one who was sacrificed for us. Christ is the one priest of the new covenant whose self-sacrifice for the sins of all has reconciled humanity to the Father. It is through this unrepeatable sacrifice, intrinsically related to the incarnation, and to Jesus's life, resurrection and ascension, that the new, holy humanity has been formed. It is this sacrifice which is celebrated and proclaimed in all its completeness, as the Church shares in Christ in the Eucharist. Significantly, there is a large measure of current ecumenical agreement that in the memorial (*anamnesis*) of the Eucharist the benefits of the once-for-all event of salvation become effective in the present through the action of the Holy Spirit.[2]

to share in Christ in the Eucharist is not only to receive him as the Father's gift to us but also to share in his offering of our human nature ... in the Eucharist we are offered by Christ to the Father

4.4   To share in Christ in the Eucharist is not only to receive him as the Father's gift to us but also to share in his offering of our human nature (and us) to the Father, and to share in his offering of us to the world. Christ's 'self-offering is not only a sacrifice of expiation and propitiation; it is at the same time the sanctifying and offering of our sinful human nature to God.'[3] In making us sharers in himself, we are given to participate in his self-offering to the Father, not only of himself *for us* but of us *with* himself. This is not to suggest that there can be any repetition or prolongation of, or addition to the once-for-all expiatory and propitiatory sacrifice of Christ. But neither is it sufficient to speak merely of our grateful response to the sacrifice of Calvary or the self-offering of our whole lives. A simple contrast between atoning sacrifice and our sacrifice of praise will be insufficient, for this bypasses Christ's continuing risen, human ministry. Stemming from the particular and unrepeatable self-offering in which the Son of God has assumed our humanity, purged it of its sin and re-created it, in the Eucharist, we, the first-fruits of his death and resurrection, are offered by Christ to the Father. 'In the action of the eucharist Christ is truly present to share his risen life with us and to unite us with himself in his self-offering to the Father, the one full, perfect and sufficient sacrifice which he alone can offer and has offered once for all.'[4] This, of course, includes the sacrifice of praise and thanksgiving – but our praise and thanksgiving are taken and borne up to the Father by, in and through Christ.

to share in Christ's ministry entails being offered by him to the world

4.5   At the same time, to share in the risen ministry of Christ in the Eucharist entails being offered by Christ to the world as Spirit-filled believers, as 'living sacrifices' (Romans 12. 1).[5] The Eucharist, precisely because it entails participation in Christ's self-offering to the Father, involves being sent out in sacrificial obedience and witness to the world.

anticipation of the new heaven and new earth in the Eucharist brings an ethical mandate to live in the world today as instruments of that promised future

4.6   At the Eucharist the people are led to proclaim the Lord's death in anticipation of the completion of God's purposes at the end of time (1 Corinthians 11. 26). We are 'opened to the past of Christ which bears upon our present, and so we are made to remember – and in that remembering, to encounter at the same time the promise of God's future in him.'[6] In celebrating, enjoying and experiencing the new covenant established by the broken body and poured out blood of Christ, the Church is granted an anticipation of the final fulfilment of the divine purposes for the entire creation. 'Because of our regular celebration of the Eucharist, the future is no stranger to us.'[7] The earliest pictures of eucharistic celebrations tell of eschatological exaltation amidst the experience of the in-breaking of the Spirit of the last days (Acts 2. 46). It is possible that Hebrews 12. 18–24, which pictures the recipients of the letter as having come to the heavenly Jerusalem, is alluding to the Eucharist. If so, in the eucharistic celebration, they are to see themselves as already having come to the final gathering of the saints 'enrolled in heaven.' Anticipation of the new heaven and new earth in the Eucharist brings to the celebration not only a joy that the world's final fulfilment is assured but also a longing for it to arrive (*Maranatha* – 'Come, Lord Jesus'), and an ethical mandate to live in the world today as instruments of that promised future.[8]

the invocation of the Holy Spirit is best understood as focused on the whole life of God's people

4.7   This participation in Christ's past, present and future is made possible by the Holy Spirit. The *epiclesis* – the invocation of the Holy Spirit – is thus a crucial part of the eucharistic action. It is best understood not as focused narrowly on the elements of bread and wine and a supposed 'moment' of consecration, but on the whole life of God's people as expressed in the entire eucharistic action, to sanctify both us and the bread and wine, so that in our corporate eating and drinking we may be united with Christ. As the Spirit binds us to Christ in his offering of himself to the Father, we are directed back to the once-made sacrifice of Christ, his victory over sin and evil. But in being drawn back we are also pointed forwards: the Spirit unites us to the risen and ascended Christ who is yet to come and brings about here and now a foretaste of God's final kingdom. 'The invocation of the Spirit on the whole eucharistic action is a pledge of the transformation of the communicants, and also the transformation of all creation, as gifts of God's creation become our spiritual food.'[9]

the Eucharist is borne along by a fundamentally trinitarian dynamic, most evident in the Thanksgiving and Communion

4.8   Thus it will be clear, then, that the Eucharist is borne along by a fundamentally trinitarian dynamic: 'eucharistic theology should be seen within the wider context of Trinitarian theology.'[10] We are drawn into the life of the Trinity, and in being drawn in are sent out from the Eucharist to partake of the triune God's mission to the world. In the liturgy, the trinitarian character of the Eucharist is perhaps most evident at two critical points: in the Thanksgiving, when the Church prays to the Father for the gift of the Son by the work of the Spirit; and in the Communion, when we participate in Christ (1 Corinthians 10. 16), which, as we have seen, is made possible by being pervaded by the Spirit and entails being led closer to the Father.

Eucharist and Church

the Eucharist is not an event for the autonomous believer, but the Church's participation in the Trinity's life

4.9   Bearing in mind these theological dimensions, especially the trinitarian aspects of the Eucharist, we can now speak more fully of the relation between the Eucharist and the Church. Given the close relation between the Trinity and the Church we have highlighted in the last two chapters, it is not surprising to find in the New Testament that the Lord's Supper, with its strong trinitarian currents, is understood in a highly corporate way. In 1 Corinthians, for example, Paul makes it clear that it is intrinsically a communal event. Indeed, there can be no Lord's Supper unless the Church is assembling as one community in such a way that all dissension, selfishness and party spirit are put aside (1 Corinthians 11. 17-34). The Eucharist is not an event for the autonomous believer, but the Church's participation in the Trinity's life, in which context the individual worshipper finds his or her place.

'we are one single body, for we all share in the one loaf': the saving reality which Christ brings includes the communion he makes possible between members of his body – the Eucharist makes the Church visible

4.10   Further, it is an event in which the identity of the Church is not simply expressed but actualised. The Anglican-Reformed Report, *God's Reign and Our Unity*, states that: 'we must say that the Eucharist is constitutive of the Church because in it Christ unites the disciples with himself.'[11] Here the 'many' are enfolded into Christ's 'one' community. In baptism, we are ingrafted into Christ's Church by the Spirit and acknowledged as children of the Father. In the Eucharist, the baptised community is nourished and renewed in its corporate life through union with Christ and the Father through the Spirit. Hans Conzelmann claims that in 1 Corinthians 10 and 11 'Paul is aiming at an interpretation of the community by means of the Last Supper'.[12] The primary category is *koinonia* – 'common participation' (C. K. Barrett) in the one bread and one cup. 'And as there is one loaf, so we, although there are many of us, are one single body, for we all share in the one loaf.' (1 Corinthians 10. 17). When the Church gathers to celebrate the Lord's Supper it shares in Christ's body, both in the sense that it partakes of his saving reality and in the sense it shares the life of Christ's new community. Indeed, the saving reality which Christ brings includes the communion he makes possible between members of his body. The Eucharist is thus not simply expressive of our *koinonia* with one another but formative of it. It is a means through which we are given to participate in the relationships and responsibilities of the Church in a particularly intense way. Extending the same point, we can say that the Eucharist makes the Church visible. This is certainly true for Paul – the many are *seen* to belong to each other by 'common participation' in the one bread and cup.[13]

not only the particular, worshipping congregation but the universal Church

4.11   As the Eucharist renews our union with Christ, it is the pledge and guarantee of our union with all who are in Christ. The Church which the Eucharist expresses, actualises and makes visible is not only the particular, worshipping congregation but the universal Church: 'eucharistic celebrations have always to do with the whole Church, and the whole Church is involved in each local eucharistic celebration'.[14] As we have suggested already, in the Eucharist the Church celebrates the communion of saints and prays for the final gathering together of all in Christ.

in the Eucharist, the Spirit re-constitutes the Church

4.12   All this coheres with our earlier discussion of the Church being constituted through the Spirit. The Holy Spirit binds the Church to the crucified and risen Christ and through him to the Father, and in so doing the members of the Church are united to one another and to all others who are 'in Christ'. And in this activity of the Spirit there is an anticipation of the final coming of the Kingdom: the future communal life of God's people is known in the present. This is the movement of the Spirit at the heart of the Eucharist. In the Eucharist, the Spirit *re-constitutes* the Church: when we share this feast, the Spirit, anticipating the final communion of all things with the triune God, repeatedly constitutes our communion with Christ and the Father, and our communion with others who are one with Christ.

it is fitting to regard the Eucharist as the fullest and richest act of worship available to the Christian community

4.13   This is not to say that the Spirit re-constitutes the Church *exclusively* in the Eucharist. The Spirit blows where he wills. It is clear that today and in the past in many parts of the Anglican Communion, including the Church of England, Christians have been built up through Morning and Evening Prayer, and in other non-sacramental services, with infrequent communion. Nevertheless, we can maintain that there is an intensity and specificity about the Eucharist.[15] Here our corporate communion with God the Trinity is crystallised and focused, thus making it fitting to regard the Eucharist as the fullest and richest act of worship available to the Christian community.

to speak of the Eucharist in such a positive way need not downplay or threaten the place of the Ministry of the Word

4.14   To speak of the Eucharist in such a positive way need not, as it might be supposed, downplay or threaten the place of the Ministry of the Word.[16] Both the Ministry of the Word and the Ministry of the Sacrament have their actualisation in the active presence of the risen Christ, in whose life we participate. Moreover, as the Church of England has always maintained, word and sacrament cannot be driven apart, for it is the word of the Gospel, testified above all in Holy Scripture, which gives the sacrament its very meaning. The Eucharist, therefore, properly includes the reading of Scripture, its proclamation and its reception by the people in faith through the Spirit. The liturgy also mediates the word of the Gospel in the words which accompany the sacrament, supremely those of the thanksgiving and memorial. Further, the sacrament mediates the word of the Gospel in the whole sacramental action, including the corporate sharing of the elements. The sacrament is the visible enactment of the Gospel-word in our midst. We recall Paul's words: 'whenever you eat this bread and drink this cup, you proclaim the Lord's death until he comes.' (1 Corinthians 11. 26)

The Eucharist and the four marks of the Church

at the Eucharist, the identity of the Church is expressed, actualised and made visible in its four marks

4.15   Pulling these strands together, we can say that *at the Eucharist, the identity of the Church is expressed, actualised and made visible in its four marks – its oneness, holiness, catholicity and apostolicity*. With regard to the Church's unity, here the 'many' who make up the body are brought together by 'common participation' in the one bread and cup, to share in Christ and the reconciling benefits of his death. With regard to the Church's holiness, here the Church is bound in dedication to the triune God, sharing in God's holiness through the holy, sanctified humanity of Jesus Christ given for us on the cross. With regard to the Church's catholicity, in this meal God demonstrates and makes available his open, unconditional love for all, sealed in Jesus Christ, and here the local Church is united in a living way with the universal Church. With regard to the Church's apostolicity, here the Church is directed back to the foundational saving history of Jesus Christ celebrated by the apostles, and discovers its calling as the body sent out into the world, to be the royal priesthood in the context of daily life, anticipating the final consummation of the whole creation.

The people as the subject of the Eucharist

for early Christian communities, active participation in worship by every member of the congregation appears to have been understood as the norm

4.16   We have already said that all members of the Church share equally in the one priesthood of Christ, and thus in the one priesthood of the Church. The New Testament makes it clear that in corporate worship, there can be no ranking of the participants with respect to their relation to God. It would seem that the event of worship for the early Christian communities was typically an experience of the immediacy of God's presence to the whole Christian community through the power of the eschatological Spirit in their midst. Active participation in worship by every member of the congregation appears to have been understood as the norm (1 Corinthians 12 and 14). In the Epistle to the Ephesians, temple imagery is used to demonstrate that the liturgical divisions of the past have been overcome in Christ. The old temple placed different categories of people in different degrees of relation to God's presence, but the new temple is formed in the new humanity of Christ and through him we all have access to the Father by the Spirit (Ephesians 2. 18). In the Epistle to the Hebrews we are told that whereas before only the high priest was allowed to enter the inner court of the temple, and then only once a year bearing the blood of sacrifice in his hands, now Christ has opened the way into the sanctuary of God's presence because by the offering of his body 'he has achieved the eternal perfection of all who are sanctified' (Hebrews 10. 14).[17]

'the assembly is the celebrant of the Eucharist'

4.17   This equality of access and status applies as much to the Eucharist as to any other act of the Church's worship and is enshrined in the liturgies of the Church of England. The worshipping congregation is the subject of the eucharistic act, sharing together in the high priesthood of Christ. Accordingly, among the principles and recommendations adopted by IALC–5 was that 'In, through, and with Christ, the assembly is the celebrant of the Eucharist.'[18]

there is differentiation of role within the one life of the Church as it shares in the life of a differentiated Trinity: so it is with eucharistic worship

4.18   Many revisions of prayer books throughout the Anglican Communion demonstrate the recovery of a sense of the manifold ministries of the people of God within the eucharistic celebration. Among these, primary are the functions which belong to the congregation as a whole – the people are called to 'gather and greet one another in the Lord's name, to hear God's word, to pray for the world, to offer the sacrifice of praise and thanksgiving, and to share the eucharistic meal.'[19] However, different members of the worshipping body will exercise different ministries. As we have observed, there is differentiation of role within the one life of the Church as it shares in the life of a differentiated Trinity. Each person is gifted by the Spirit in a particular way to perform a particular task within the liturgical life of the Church, the primary aim being the good of the whole body (1 Corinthians 12). So it is with eucharistic worship. Some of these particular ministries are representative, performed on behalf of the whole body (for example, the bringing of the elements to the table and the gathering of alms and oblations), while others arise from particular gifts that individuals have received (for example, singing, reading). The former can be exercised by any baptised member of the congregation. However, the latter need to be recognised by the community – for example, not everyone is a capable reader – and need to be co-ordinated by the leadership.

Eucharistic presidency: historical considerations

it may be assumed that the first Christian community leaders took over a role similar to that of the ruler of the synagogue

4.19   The particular eucharistic ministry surrounded by most controversy is that of presidency. Clearly, worship needs some kind of steering and guiding. The proper ordering of worship was seen as a clear requirement of the early Church (1 Corinthians 14. 40), especially in the light of potential chaos of charismatic worship and the inherited experience of leadership in Jewish worship. It may reasonably be assumed that the first Christian community leaders took over a role similar to that of the *archisunagogos* (ruler of the synagogue) in contemporary Jewish worship. The holders of this office were often communal benefactors and patrons, but their functions could include the maintenance of order and the supervision of the conduct of the synagogue assembly.[20] There is a vital distinction to bear in mind here between presidency proper (that is, oversight and direction of the synagogue's liturgy), and the actual leading of the worship itself. The ruler of the synagogue could act as a kind of chairman of the proceedings but he did not have any liturgical functions which were his exclusive prerogative. For example, he could invite any competent person to lead the prayers, read and expound the Scriptures and no special qualifications were required for these tasks.

it is probable that the elders who seem to have been assigned to take responsibility for the community took part in the leadership of worship

4.20 Evidence about the role in worship of the earliest Christian community-leaders is extremely sparse. It appears that there were those with particular gifts to lead and to care and in these cases there seems to have been the natural assumption of responsibility, without any formal appointment procedure, on the basis that appropriate gifts of leadership had been displayed and discerned. There are indications, as we have noted, that a major element in the gifts they were expected to have was the ability to 'speak the word of God' in some form. It may be supposed that they themselves would have taken a prominent part in the liturgical Ministry of the Word as well as overseeing the contributions to the worship made by other members of the community. It is probable that the elders (*presbuteroi*) who seem to have been assigned to take responsibility for the community (Acts 14. 23, 15. 23, 20. 17; Titus 1. 5; James 5. 17) took part in the leadership of worship. And it is possible that these two types of leader were (or became) the same people, as the phrase 'presiding elders' (*proestotes presbuteroi*) of 1 Timothy 5. 17 suggests – their gifts being acknowledged by their appointment to an office.

there is no suggestion in the New Testament that anyone was ordained to an office which consisted primarily of saying the blessing over the bread and wine

4.21 However, as far as eucharistic presidency is concerned, there is no indication anywhere in the New Testament of an explicit link between the Church's office and presiding at the Eucharist. There is certainly no attempt to link theologically the discernment of charismatic gifts and the developing notions of office with particular powers, functions or responsibilities with respect to the Eucharist. There is no suggestion that anyone was ordained or appointed to an office which consisted primarily of saying the blessing over the bread and wine.

it would be a mistake to jump to the conclusion that eucharistic presidency was, in principle, open to anyone

4.22   The significance of this silence is severely limited, however, by the restricted scope of the New Testament source material. First, there is an extreme sparsity of unambiguous reference to the Eucharist in the New Testament. Paul's references to the cup, the bread, and the Lord's Supper in 1 Corinthians 10 and 11 are the only passages which purport to describe early Christian eucharistic practice at any length, and even these references are brief. When the breaking of bread is mentioned incidentally and very briefly in Acts, it is not always clear that the Eucharist is in view. Secondly, the functions associated with church offices in the New Testament have to be gathered from general references to superintendence, teaching, and pastoral care by *episcopoi* and *presbuteroi*; the qualifications of character and repute required in office holders are listed, but not the specific functions pertaining to each office. It would therefore be a mistake to jump from the silence of these severely limited sources to the conclusion that the eucharistic presidency was, in principle, open to anyone.

a competent person is required; there was a need for proper ordering; saying the Eucharistic Prayer would have fallen to someone with the gift of proclamation

4.23   Against that background, three more particular considerations deserve notice. First, it might be argued that because in Jewish worship the ruler of the synagogue could invite any competent member of the congregation to lead the prayers, read and expound the Scriptures, anyone in the congregation might be called upon to say the eucharistic prayers in a Christian assembly. But it should be remembered that a *competent* person is required, and competence in the case of eucharistic prayer implies suitability to pronounce the blessings at a communal meal. On the analogy of ancient Jewish meal-blessings, pronounced by the head of a household, we might expect the suitable eucharistic president to be someone of high standing in the community. Second, there was a clear need for the proper ordering and guiding of the community's worship and this would naturally fall to the pastoral leader(s) of the community. Third, since the Eucharistic Prayer had to be improvised and essentially involved the recounting of the mighty acts of God, it is again natural to suppose that it would have fallen to someone with the gift of proclamation – one of the leaders would have been the obvious choice. All this would suggest that the presidency of the Eucharist was not left to anyone; it is more likely that it was undertaken by those who were the leaders of a particular gathering.

evolving liturgies demonstrate both that the New Testament emphasis on the people as the subject of the eucharistic action remained, and at the same time, the requirement for someone to preside became more clearly expressed

4.24   In the second, third and fourth centuries, the surviving examples of the evolving liturgies of the Church demonstrate both that the New Testament emphasis on the people as the subject of the eucharistic action remained, and at the same time, the requirement for someone to preside over the eucharistic event became more clearly expressed.[21] However, there seems to have been considerable fluidity as to who could assume this presiding function. The *Didache* (first century AD) refers to prophets, apostles and teachers. Clement (c. 96) mentions presbyters and bishops (without distinguishing between them). Ignatius (c. 110) believes a valid Eucharist is only possible by restricting presidency to the bishop or those specifically delegated by him (without indicating whether or not they are presbyters). Tertullian (early third century) opposed lay presidency in his earlier works, not least from a desire to maintain good order. When he later allied himself to the Montanist schism, he accepted the view that since the baptised are already priests, not only might they exercise priestly functions, but they should also accept priestly discipline (e.g. monogamy).[22] Cyprian (early third century) regards the bishop as the normal eucharistic president, but his priesthood is on occasion shared by the presbyters. The *Apostolic Tradition* of Hippolytus (c. 215) envisages bishops but also allows 'confessors', who had not received the laying on of hands, to preside. It also appears deacons were presiding in some places before the Council of Arles in 314 disallowed the practice.

a common thread was that 'those who preside over the life of the Church preside at the Eucharist'

4.25   Despite this diversity, a common thread in this period was that oversight of the community and presidency at the Eucharist belonged together. This was not because of any particular powers which were thought to be concentrated in the president but because presidency at the Eucharist was the liturgical expression or outworking of the pastoral responsibility which was laid upon him as a leader of the Church. Hervé-Marie Legrand is one of a number of scholars to stress this:

> with all the witnesses we note that it is a fact, and most often it is axiomatic (Clement, Ignatius, Justin, Tertullian, Hippolytus, Cyprian and the canonical tradition deriving from Hippolytus), that *those who preside over the life of the Church preside at the Eucharist.*
>
> (Legrand (1979), p. 425)

from the post-apostolic period, perceptions of the eucharist president changed

4.26   From the post-apostolic period onwards, however, for a variety of reasons, the way in which the president was perceived and perceived himself underwent substantial changes,[23] loosening the ties between eucharistic presidency and pastoral oversight. To begin with, we can trace a marked shift from a situation in which 'charism' (manifest gifting) played a major part to one in which 'office' was almost entirely determinative, in particular, the office of bishop and those whom he appointed.[24] This brought with it a clericalism of liturgical functions and a decided shift from corporate to individual eucharistic celebration. The *Didache* seems to presuppose a situation in which 'bishops' and 'deacons' are being appointed to Churches over and above the more obviously gifted leaders they already knew and accepted. There is some evidence that such formally appointed community-leaders began to claim, by virtue of their appointment, the same *charismata* as those which their predecessors possessed – their office was seen as conferring charism. With Hippolytus there also appears to be a strong link between appointment and the bestowal of *charismata*. Clement believes there are strict rules governing the presidency of the Eucharist which limit this function to those properly ordained, which he takes to exclude 'laymen' (the first known use of the term by a Christian writer). Ignatius provides the earliest evidence we have of the office of a bishop as the leader of a body of presbyters in charge of a local Church. He argues that authority over the Christian community should rest with the bishop. As with Clement, in the last analysis it is the possession of office and not the external manifestation of *charismata* which is to be the decisive factor in assessing who is to be regarded as the true minister of the Church. So for Ignatius, only those celebrations of the Eucharist, baptisms, and agapes are to be regarded as genuine which are presided over by the bishop or one whom he has delegated.

bishops laid claim to liturgical acts, and brought to an end much of the active participation of the whole people of God

4.27   Neither Clement nor Ignatius should necessarily be taken as representing the orthodoxy of the time, but their views did come to be espoused by the later Church. In due course, the presidency of all liturgical assemblies was entirely taken over by the bishop, who continued to improvise the Eucharistic Prayer as his 'charismatic' predecessors had done. Not only this, the bishops increasingly laid claim to various liturgical acts which had originally been exercised by others – indeed, he became chief minister of both word and sacrament and this eventually brought to an end much of the active participation of the whole people of God in leading worship which had been such a marked feature of primitive Christianity.

in the fourth century, bishops began to delegate local pastoral functions to presbyters

4.28   This growing stress on the episcopal office and the gradual attraction of all major liturgical functions to the bishop did not preclude episcopal delegation. It seems that it in the fourth century, bishops with an increasingly regional ministry began to delegate local pastoral functions to presbyters, and from this period they come to be regarded as possessing certain inherent liturgical functions by virtue of their office, which were consequently denied to the diaconate and the laity. From this time we see a growing consciousness that presbyters celebrating the Eucharist together with the bishop are doing something that the laity cannot do, something only they have the mandate to perform.

in succeeding centuries, the connection between a local community and the ordained ministry was threatened

4.29   The further development in the succeeding centuries of these tendencies is well known. The connection between a local community and the ordained ministry was seriously threatened by defining the bishop and priest/presbyter essentially in terms of a juridical connection with Christ through historic succession and the endowment of a personal power or mark which in some way belonged to the individual (indelibly) and in practical isolation from the rest of the community.

there was a growth of distinctive uses of the language of priesthood and sacrifice in relation to eucharistic presidency . . . a situation was encouraged where the offering at the hands of the priest could be seen as taking on a distinctive role of its own

4.30   Bound up with these developments, and contributing towards them, was the growth of distinctive uses of the language of priesthood and sacrifice in relation to eucharistic presidency. The word-group 'priest' (*hiereus*) is used of Christ and collectively of the Church, but never an individual minister in the New Testament (apart from Romans 15. 16, where Paul speaks of his 'priestly ministry [*hierourgounta to euangelion*] of the Gospel of God'). Before the end of the second century, Tertullian uses *sacerdos* (Latin, 'priest') as the ordinary word for bishop. For Cyprian, a few decades later, the bishop is seen as the normal eucharistic president, sharing his priesthood on occasion with his presbyters. (It was rare in the ancient Church, however, for a presbyter to preach or preside at the Eucharist.) As early as the end of the first century, the eucharistic action is being spoken of in terms of offering sacrifice. In Irenaeus (late second century), the core of the 'sacrifice' offered in the Eucharist was that of thanks and praise to God, an offering made in the presenting to him of the bread and wine, and the prayer of thanksgiving over them. But this sacrificial language was capable of being developed through linking *this* offering with the sacrifice of Christ, leading eventually to the conviction that Christ is in some sense offered to God. The extension of this family of ideas into medieval eucharistic theology has been well charted. The doctrine of eucharistic sacrifice, eventually reinforced by the doctrine of transubstantiation, had a marked effect on the way the ordained priesthood was understood. The belief that the sacrifice itself is present at the Mass (the same that was offered to God on Calvary, for Christ is present as victim and priest); the conviction that the priest acts on earth *in persona Christi*, as Christ's representative; the notion that the priest alone – by virtue of the office and status conferred by ordination – possesses the power to effect the transformation of the substance of the elements into the substance of the body and blood of Christ, together encouraged a situation where the offering at the hands of the priest, though regarded as wholly dependent on Christ's self-offering, could nevertheless be seen as taking on a distinctive role of its own and be understood as sacrificial in its own right, effecting 'satisfaction' and even 'placating' God on behalf of the living and the dead.

there is a marked move away from the notion of a person suitably gifted in pastoral oversight presiding over a rite celebrated corporately by the whole Church, to the idea of the priest doing something instead of the people

4.31   Clearly, this account omits a vast amount of detail, and could easily suggest (wrongly) a universal and steady deterioration of eucharistic theology and practice in the medieval era. We have only been able to trace some significant developments. The general observation to be made here is that from a very early date in the Church's life there is a marked move away from the notion of a person suitably gifted in pastoral oversight presiding over a rite celebrated corporately by the whole Church, to the idea of the priest doing something instead of the people (albeit for their benefit). This tendency towards the isolation of priest and laity was strengthened, among other things, by the continued use of Latin in the West after it had ceased to be used by most of the laity, the saying of the consecration or canon silently, the infiltration of the priest's private devotions into the rite, and the restriction of communion to one kind (the bread only) for the laity.

the Reformation doctrine of the 'priesthood of all believers' meant a corporate sharing in the one and unique priesthood of Jesus Christ

4.32   The ferment of the Protestant Reformation led to a widespread questioning of these developments. Martin Luther, for example, not only subjected the doctrine of transubstantiation to radical criticism, but insisted that in the New Testament the authority and dignity of priesthood resided in the community of believers. There is one spiritual estate in which all have freedom of access to God's presence. All who are united to Christ by baptism and through faith share in Christ's priestly work of intercession and instruction, praise and proclamation. Although the theme of 'the priesthood of all believers' was not so prominent in the writings of the other mainstream reformers, the theological content of the doctrine became foundational for all Reformation theology. It is important to stress that although Luther delighted in declaring that all Christians are priests, he did not do so to encourage individualistic ideas of independence but to stress the fact of our corporate interdependence. Fundamentally, the Reformation doctrine of the 'priesthood of all believers' meant a *corporate* sharing in the one and unique priesthood of Jesus Christ.

the reformers drew a distinction between the priesthood which is the 'common property of all Christians' and the office to which particular persons are called

4.33   None the less, Luther, with other mainline reformers, drew a distinction between personal status and public office. There is the priesthood which is the 'common property of all Christians' and the office of the Church to which particular persons are called by the community. The community calls out individuals to minister in word and sacrament for the sake of the good order of the Church. This ministry is exercised only by the consent of the Christian community, who can reject the minister's claims to authority if they find him unfaithful to the Gospel.[25]

for Luther, ordination bestows the functions of public preaching of the word, the administration of the sacraments, and the power of the keys

4.34   For Luther the only distinction between priests and laity is that of 'office' or 'function' and the 'work' or 'responsibility' with which they are entrusted. Ordination is not about status or a change of 'being'; it is about a congregation permitting individuals to carry out the office and work of a priest. This questioning of the distinction in anything other than function between a priest and layperson undercut medieval conceptions of the sacrifice of the Mass and the distinctively sacrificial role of the priest. Nevertheless, though the power and privilege to celebrate the Eucharist is 'given to all', the task of presiding should be placed with those who are called to be responsible for the spiritual health of the community. Ordination bestows the functions of public preaching of the word, the administration of the sacraments, and the power of the keys. If someone is recognised by the community as having the right to preach the gospel, that person also ought to have the right to preside at the Eucharist.

the reformers' conviction was that the sacraments are subordinate to the proclamation and reception of the word

4.35   Behind this lay a conviction to be found in all the mainline reformers about the intimate connection between word and sacrament. Ministers are ordained to the ministry of word and sacrament, and both convey the evangelical promises of grace. The sacraments must not be allowed to take on a life of their own for they are subordinate to the proclamation and reception of the word. The case which the mainstream reformers made for restricting the Ministry of the Sacrament to appointed ministers rests ultimately on their understanding of the indissolubility of word and sacrament, and the dependence of the latter on the former. The Ministry of the Word is made available and applied to the life of the Church only through authorised, ordained ministers – so it should be with the sacraments.

characteristics of the English reformers:

4.36   As far as the English reformers are concerned, a number of key characteristics of their eucharistic theology and theology of ordination should be emphasised.

1: they allowed nothing to detract from the uniqueness of Christ's priesthood

4.37   First, for them nothing was to be allowed to detract from the uniqueness of Christ's priesthood. Thomas Cranmer, for example, believed that to treat the Lord's Supper as an offering to the Father to plead remission of sins for the living and the dead is to dishonour the priesthood of Christ; we participate in Christ's sacrifice and its fruits. The only offering from our side is the self-offering of the people in thanksgiving and praise for the benefits received.

2: the Eucharist was the meal of the whole Church

4.38   Second, the Eucharist was the meal of the *whole* Church. Cranmer declares that 'all remember Christ's death, all give thanks to God, and repent and offer themselves an oblation to Christ, all take him for their Lord and Saviour, and spiritually feed upon him.'[26]

3: ministerial office and the Church community were inseparable

4.39   Third, like other Reformed ordinals, the early Anglican rites put considerable stress on the inseparability of ministerial office and the Church community. This was brought out partly by the requirement (in the Preface to the 1550 Ordinal) that candidates for ordination be duly tried and tested, partly by their public interrogation by the bishop, and partly by the requirement that ordinations should be 'upon a Sunday or holyday, in the face of the church'.

4: ordination was linked to the universal Church

4.40   Fourth, ordination was seen as integrally related not only to a local community but to the universal Church. The retention of episcopal ordination – the bishop representing the catholic Church – bears witness to this.

5: though retaining the word 'priest', the ordinals reject the notion of sacrificial priesthood linked to the eucharistic offering

4.41   Fifth, the ordinals reject the notion of sacrificial priesthood as linked to the eucharistic offering by the late medieval Church in favour of a pastoral and didactic model of the ordained priesthood centring on public proclamation (the Ministry of the Word), the administration of the sacraments, and private exhortation. However, although deeply influenced by their continental counterparts, the English reformers chose to retain the word 'priest' for the second order of ministry, partly out of respect for tradition, partly out of a concern to distinguish the second order of minister from the third, partly to avoid the implications of a presbyterian form of government, and on the understanding that 'priest' was an equivalent term to the Greek *presbuteros* ('presbyter'). The use of the word 'priest' has been retained by the Anglican tradition in common with the larger part of Christendom.

6: a heavy stress on the Ministry of the Word in relation to ordination

4.42   Sixth, we find the same heavy stress on the Ministry of the Word in relation to ordination, in line with the continental reformers. In the pre-Reformation Sarum rite, the candidate for priesthood was handed a chalice and/or paten as symbols of priestly office with the words 'Receive the power to offer sacrifice to God', whereas in the 1552 English Ordinal, the Bible alone is given, accompanied by the words 'Take thou authority to preach the Word of God, and to minister the holy sacraments in the congregation.'

Eucharistic presidency: some conclusions

the president's role is to ensure that the whole people together properly celebrate the sacrament

4.43   It is time to draw together some conclusions about eucharistic presidency, bearing in mind the affirmations of the opening section of this chapter (4.2–4.15), and the historical horizons we have just opened up, especially those of the English Reformation. If we take seriously the Eucharist as the feast at which the whole people of God are the celebrants, the president's role is not to do something instead of the people, but (as Cranmer was so keen to stress) *to ensure that the whole people together properly celebrate the sacrament*. The presider's role is not simply to lead the service but to lead in service – that is, to enable the people to fulfil their vocation on this occasion as Christ's body sharing in Christ's priesthood.

the president is to attend to key theological dimensions

4.44   If this is so, the president is to *attend to the theological dimensions we opened up at the beginning of this chapter* (4.2–4.8). He or she is to ensure as far as possible that there is a genuine sharing in Christ by the people, that there is particular (though not exclusive) attention paid to the sacrificial death of Christ, that there is a participation in the risen Christ's offering of our human nature (and us) to the Father and his offering of us to the world, that there is an anticipation of the completion of God's purposes, and that there is a sense of the community being invited by the Spirit in the trinitarian communion of God.

the eucharistic president is to be a sign and focus of the unity, holiness, catholicity and apostolicity of the Church

4.45   In 4.15, we concluded that, given these theological dimensions of the Eucharist (especially its trinitarian dimensions), and tracing the close connection between Church and Eucharist in the New Testament, it is reasonable to claim that at the Eucharist the identity of the Church is expressed, actualised and made visible in its four marks in an especially intensive way. Accordingly, we would suggest that *the eucharistic president is to be a sign and focus of the unity, holiness, catholicity and apostolicity of the Church, and the one who has primary responsibility for ensuring that the Church's four marks are expressed, actualised and made visible in the eucharistic celebration.*

the restriction of eucharistic presidency to those ordained as bishop or priest/ presbyter brings assurance that this ministry is being performed by one who not only is closely related to the local community of Christians, but also is a minister of the Church universal

4.46   If this is so, it would seem distinctly appropriate, to put it no stronger for the moment, that presidency over the community's celebration of the Eucharist belongs to those with overall pastoral oversight of the community, i.e. to those ordained as bishop or priest/presbyter. For eucharistic presidency is an intensive form of the presbyter's role in relation to the community, which, we have contended, is to 'promote, release and clarify' the many ministries of the Church 'in such a way that the other ministries can exemplify and sustain the four "marks" of the Church – its oneness, holiness, catholicity and apostolicity' (3.26). In relation to apostolicity, this may include standing over against the community as well as being part of it (3.34). The restriction of eucharistic presidency to those ordained as bishop or priest/presbyter, which is (as we have said) an intensive form of the presbyter's role in relation to the community, brings assurance that this ministry is being performed by one who not only is closely related to the local community of Christians, but also is a minister of the Church universal. It also brings assurance that this ministry is being performed by a presbyter who has received the sign of historic episcopal succession. We note that many ecumenical statements have stressed the inseparability of presiding over the community and presiding at the Eucharist,[27] and this is thoroughly in line with the practice, as far as it can be discerned, of the earliest Christian communities. As IALC–5 put it in one of its joint recommendations, 'The liturgical functions of the ordained arise out of pastoral responsibility. Separating liturgical function and pastoral oversight tends to reduce liturgical presidency to an isolated ritual function.'[28] To express the last sentence in another way, separating liturgical function and pastoral oversight runs the risk of inhibiting the realisation of the four marks of the Church.

eucharistic presidency does not mean performing every liturgical ministry

4.47   As we have indicated above (1.4–1.9) eucharistic presidency does not mean performing every liturgical ministry. Some ministries in the liturgical assembly are directly related to gifts; this is most obviously true of musicians and those who read and lead prayer. Other parts are properly the responsibility of the whole assembly, who may very well delegate these functions to lay rather than ordained members. Such actions include reading scripture, intercession, the bringing of gifts and distribution of Holy Communion.

diaconal ministry has developed

4.48   Diaconal ministry has developed in two directions; in serving the assembly by ordering its response, and in freeing the president to lead the worship. For example, the deacon shapes the various petitions for prayer brought and offered by individuals in the assembly into a coherent whole and gives practical directions to help the smooth flow of the liturgy – hymn numbers as well as the dismissal. The deacon models the incarnational pattern of Christ the servant in such a way as reading the gospel ('the Word was made flesh and dwelt among us') and preparing the table ('the Son of man came not to be served, but to serve').

the presidency of a bishop or priest gives a clarity of focus

4.49   The bishop, or the presbyter who presides in his stead, presides over the whole rite, as note 2 in ASB Rite A (p. 115) makes clear. This is a sign that word and sacrament are not divided, but together reveal God's saving activity and invite the assembly's renewed response with the consequent transformation that it brings. The presidency of a bishop or priest ordained for the service of the universal Church gives a clarity of focus which signifies that the Eucharist is an act of the one Christ in his Church, the feast of God to which we are invited, not a buffet from which we help ourselves.

it is because the bishop (or presbyter) represents the point at which Christ's unity is focused in the assembly that the declaratory elements are presidential

4.50   The president, whether bishop or presbyter, greets the assembly with an apostolic greeting and so constitutes it as an activity of the whole Church at worship, summing up the assembly's Godward aspirations in the opening prayer or collect. In the Liturgy of the Word it is the universal Church's use of Scripture, not a local version, which is being proclaimed. There is an expectation that the one Christ will speak through the gospel. So presidents have a responsibility to see that the lectionary, rather than local preferences, governs the choice of readings. If they are not preaching themselves, they have the further responsibility to make sure that whoever does so can be trusted by the Church to discern the mind of Christ. Certain elements are presidential, in the sense that they unite the community. It is because the bishop (or presbyter) represents the point at which Christ's unity is focused in the assembly that the declaratory elements – the Greeting at the Peace, the Absolution and the Blessing – are presidential. Most significant is the Eucharistic Prayer, where the whole Church unites itself to the one perfect self-offering of Christ to the Father, identifying itself as faithful to the command of Christ – 'Do this in remembrance of me'. The prayer is the prayer of the whole assembly, but the opening dialogue and continuing interchange between presidential text and the assembly's acclamations establishes the whole as the prayer of Christ in his Church. It is this sense of the presence of Christ in his Church that the presidency of the ordained minister gives.

the bishop has traditionally been seen as pre-eminently the eucharistic president

4.51   As the ASB makes clear, when the bishop is present at a Eucharist, it is appropriate that he should act as president (even though, as the ASB stipulates, he may delegate parts of the service (32–49) to a priest if he so wishes). This is because the bishop has responsibility for the oversight of the larger community of which this particular gathering is an expression: the bishop has traditionally been seen as pre-eminently the eucharistic president, sharing his presidency with presbyters/priests.

the distribution of Holy Communion is a ministry that is properly exercised by lay people as well as clergy

4.52   As far as distribution of Holy Communion is concerned, in some Anglican dioceses this is undertaken by ordained ministers alone; in others lay people assist, while in yet others lay people are allowed to administer the chalice but not the bread. Some allow lay ministers to take consecrated elements to the sick, others do not. But the distribution of Holy Communion is a ministry that is properly exercised by lay people as well as clergy, and in this there is no justification for adopting different policies in regard to the bread and the wine.

'it would better reflect the communal nature of the Eucharist for a small group to go to the housebound person'

4.53   The point has also been made that 'When someone is prevented temporarily from joining in the worship of their local Church, as for example through sickness, it would better reflect the communal nature of the Eucharist for a small group of people to go directly from their Sunday Eucharist to the housebound person, with elements consecrated at the celebration, sharing the word, prayers, and fellowship of liturgy with them, than to provide a celebration involving that person and a presbyter alone.'[29]

5

Lay presidency?

some comments on the arguments in favour of lay presidency would seem to be necessary

5.1   At the end of the last chapter, in the light of a theological appraisal of the roles of laity and clergy at the Eucharist, we concluded that it is highly appropriate that the person who presides over the community should also do so over the eucharistic celebration. However, that conclusion requires strengthening, especially in the light of various theological arguments that are mounted to advocate lay presidency in one form or another. Although this report does not have the issue of lay presidency as its major focus of concern, as noted in the opening chapter (1.4), this is undoubtedly the most debated and currently contentious issue with regard to the respective places of clergy and laity at the Eucharist, and some comments on the arguments in favour of lay presidency, even if brief, would seem to be necessary.

no serious supporter of lay presidency is suggesting anything like a 'free for all'

5.2   We have said that 'lay presidency' can cover a range of possible schemes. It also ought to be recognised that proponents of lay presidency normally give careful attention to delineating the circumstances they feel would make it a suitable practice and the safeguards they consider necessary to ensure a properly ordered celebration. Fears about lay presidency 'opening the floodgates' and introducing anarchy in the Church are understandable, but no serious supporter of lay presidency is suggesting anything like a 'free for all' situation where anyone can assume the role of eucharistic president as they think fit.

we can offer some general responses to those who would justify lay presidency on theological grounds

5.3   Bearing in mind that this is primarily a concise theological statement, we cannot hope to engage in detail with the whole range of proposals for lay presidency. (Nor can we offer comment on the alternatives to lay presidency offered in response to what is broadly called 'pastoral necessity' (1.23). There are undoubtedly matters of enormous importance to address here but they are outside the parameters of this report.) We can, however, offer some more general responses to those who would justify lay presidency on theological grounds, assuming our minimal definition of lay presidency (1.10): the overseeing of the entire eucharistic celebration by any person who is not an episcopally ordained priest.

The supposed silence of the New Testament

the silence of the New Testament does not of itself provide grounds for opening eucharistic presidency to lay people and deacons

5.4   Supporters of lay presidency will sometimes point to the fact that the New Testament writers nowhere appear to restrict presidency at the Lord's Supper to a particular class of ministers. Indeed, the New Testament has no clear statement as to who presided. However, we remarked in Chapter 4 that we cannot conclude from this that presidency was open, in principle, to anyone during this period (4.21). The silence of the New Testament does not of itself provide grounds for opening eucharistic presidency to lay people and deacons. Apart from the relevance of countervailing factors in the Jewish background to the Lord's Supper we mentioned, deciding on the advisability of lay presidency depends primarily on attending to pivotal theological matters about which the New Testament is most definitely not silent – God, the Church, leadership, the place of the Lord's Supper in the Church and so forth – and then relating the issue of eucharistic presidency to these. This we have attempted to do in the preceding chapters.

The priesthood of all believers

defenders of lay presidency can sometimes appeal to the Reformation principle of 'the priesthood of all believers': behind this lies a critique of 'clericalisation'

5.5   Defenders of lay presidency can sometimes appeal to the Reformation principle of 'the priesthood of all believers'. To restrict the presidency of the Eucharist to episcopally ordained presbyters/priests, they claim, eclipses the equality which all believers enjoy before God by virtue of their baptism: all are priests, therefore all ought to be allowed, in principle at least, to preside at the Eucharist. Behind this line of argument lies a continuing, and to a large extent historically justified, critique of 'clericalisation' in the Church. The critique ought to be heard and its force felt. As we have seen, any suggestion of the essential separation or superiority of clergy with respect to the laity is theologically unacceptable and will undoubtedly inhibit a proper appreciation of the roles of clergy and laity at the Eucharist.

but the priesthood of all believers is properly understood as a corporate description, not an individual mandate

5.6   However, the propriety of lay presidency does not follow from the rejection of clericalisation. In fact, to argue directly from the priesthood of all believers to lay presidency can imply that it is the president who alone is priest.[1] Moreover, we have seen that the priesthood of all believers is properly understood as a corporate description, not an individual mandate. Although it includes the truth that every believer shares a common dignity through equal access to God through Christ, the main thrust of the doctrine is that the Church collectively shares in the priesthood of Christ, and it is the role of the ordained ministry to facilitate this corporate priesthood. Correctly applied to the Eucharist, then, the priesthood of all believers should remind us that the whole congregation celebrates and participates in Christ's ministry, not the priest alone. Vital as this is to keep in mind, it does not of itself say anything about widening eucharistic presidency beyond ordained priests/presbyters, only that the president must make every effort to facilitate the Church's being included in the priesthood of Christ.

nor will lay presidency necessarily reduce a sense of superiority of clergy over laity

5.7   Nor, we might add, will the introduction of lay presidency necessarily reduce a sense of division between clergy and laity, or a sense of the superiority of clergy over laity – these will only go when the distinctive roles of clergy *as members of the people of God* are identified and practised accordingly. We have attempted to show something of what this entails in the preceding chapters.

The place of the local congregation

it is felt by some that presidency is the business of the local congregation: but worshipping congregations should be seen as local manifestations of the one universal Church

5.8   It is felt by some supporters of lay presidency that the presidency of the Eucharist is the business of the local congregation, arguing that the person to preside should be chosen by the people, that the exercise of external authority or control is inappropriate, and that eucharistic presidency requires nothing more than a recognition by the local congregation that it is proper for a particular person to exercise this ministry. However, we can never afford to forget that ordination is always within and for the people of God and never apart from them. It will be clear that our case above requires worshipping congregations to be seen as integrally united to each other as local manifestations of the one universal Church. The ordained are part of networks within which the wholeness and inter-relatedness of the Church can be achieved and made visible. At the Eucharist the local Church is united in a vibrant way with the universal Church. All this would seem to point strongly in the direction of restricting presidency to priests/presbyters.

Eucharistic presidency – the centre of ordination?

the main purpose of ordination is to provide publicly recognised oversight of a community . . .

5.9   It is not uncommon to find arguments for lay presidency motivated by a desire to undermine what is felt to be a questionable assumption among some of its opponents: namely that the heart of ordination is the conferral of power or authority to preside at the Eucharist. Apart from the Absolution and Blessing, the only function strictly denied to those who are not priests is to say the Eucharistic Prayer. This not only gives that function an almost superstitious status; it is to make ordination revolve around eucharistic presidency in a quite unacceptable way. To pick up Trevor Lloyd's words: 'If one argument against lay presidency is that it would take away from the ordained man the only specific thing that is left to him alone, does that therefore imply that the main purpose of ordination is to provide eucharistic presidents?'[2] To

the bishop shares the cure of souls in a particular place with presbyters, and eucharistic presidency as exercised by them is an apt form of pastoral oversight

this question the reply must simply be 'no'. Arguments against lay presidency which suggest that ordination is exclusively or primarily about the authority or power to preside at the Eucharist are indeed misplaced. But opposition to lay presidency at the Eucharist does not necessarily entail holding this view of ordination. This should be clear from the foregoing chapters. (In any case, it is extremely unwise to try to define ordination to the presbyterate/priesthood by reference to those functions which are legally denied to others.) The main purpose of ordination is not to provide eucharistic presidents but to provide publicly recognised oversight of a community. The primary form of this in an episcopal Church is the office of bishop, combining various aspects of pastoral oversight, preaching, teaching, and guardianship of the Church's doctrine, all often expressed through his liturgical role. The bishop shares the cure of souls in a particular place with presbyters, and thus eucharistic presidency as exercised by them is also a particularly concentrated and very apt form of pastoral oversight.

The inseparability of pastoral and liturgical functions

it is eminently proper for eucharistic presidency to be restricted to those with pastoral responsibility in the sense of overall responsibility for a specific community, in other words, bishops and priests/presbyters

5.10   In the previous chapter, much was made of the inseparability of pastoral and liturgical functions. Some have used this, however, not to oppose but to *defend* lay presidency. For example, it has been said that 'there are around the world many congregations in many different social settings where a deacon or lay person holds at least some pastoral responsibility for the flock, and to have such a pastor also responsible for the provision of the Eucharist would unite the pastoral and liturgical functions'.[3] But much hinges on what is meant by the phrase 'at least some pastoral responsibility'. Our contention is that it is eminently proper for eucharistic presidency to be restricted to those with pastoral responsibility in the sense of overall responsibility for a specific community, in other words, bishops and priests/presbyters, bearing in mind that the responsibility of bishops and presbyters is also for the life of the whole Church and for the communion of local communities with one another.[4] Where lay persons (including deacons) are acting as those with such oversight, we would concur with the findings of one of the groups at the Dublin IALC gathering, namely that 'they are exercising what are essentially presbyteral functions, and therefore ought to be ordained as presbyters.'[5] If they are not, liturgical and pastoral functions are in danger of being severed, and this can only lead to confusion about the role of the ordained.[6]

a visiting priest represents the bishop, who together with the college of priests, combine pastoral and liturgical leadership within the diocese as a whole

5.11   Sometimes, of course, the converse may be the case, namely that a priest exercises eucharistic presidency without any or much pastoral responsibility. What account can be given of such circumstance? On the one hand it could be argued that, if regularly practised, it fractures the pastoral and liturgical roles we are concerned to unite; on the other hand it might be replied that a visiting priest represents the bishop who, together with the college of priests, combine pastoral and liturgical leadership within the diocese as a whole. The question how a given diocese responds to the demand of those areas of England where the provision of priests is sparse needs constantly to be addressed. We cannot overlook the fact that, even if lay presidency is disallowed, acute theological questions about the relation between liturgical and pastoral functions will often be raised by the current necessities of particular pastoral contexts.

The parity of word and sacrament

the parity of word and sacrament would appear to weigh heavily in favour of some form of lay presidency

5.12   The parity of word and sacrament would appear to weigh heavily in favour of some form of lay presidency. In its commonest form, the argument runs like this: if, as is now the case, a non-ordained person can be licensed or authorised to preach, then the same should apply to presiding at the Eucharist; the non-ordained are allowed to preach without all the training and gifts necessary for full-time pastoral oversight of the congregation; moreover, to refuse lay presidency but allow lay preaching is effectively to exalt the sacrament above the word, which as we have seen has no justification.

however, we need to be careful in drawing parallels

5.13   It is undoubtedly true that, especially with the evolution of the office of Reader, there has been a persistent tendency to allow the ministry of word and sacrament to be separated, with a consequent danger that the Ministry of the Sacrament will not be undergirded by proper training.[7] This is a matter which undoubtedly needs addressing. However, we need to be careful in drawing parallels too hastily between the ministry of word and sacrament. It needs to be recalled that teaching authority properly belongs to the ordained priest/presbyter as part of his/her ordination to the ministry of word and sacrament. This may be delegated to a lay preacher who has received appropriate preparation and training, but responsibility for or oversight of the proclamation of the Gospel still belongs to the ordained minister of a congregation.

Baptism, Eucharist and the emergency situation

another line of approach refers to what is seen as an inconsistency concerning baptism

5.14   Another line of approach refers to what is seen as an inconsistency concerning baptism. Since the first Prayer Book, the Church of England has permitted lay people and deacons to baptise in an emergency situation. Indeed, the permission of any person to baptise in an emergency is a very ancient tradition in the Church. But this provision is not made for the Eucharist. This, some claim, constitutes a serious discrepancy and might even imply that the Eucharist is in some manner superior to baptism.

in the case of baptism there was always the possibility of genuine emergency – it makes no sense to refuse baptism in a near-death situation because of the absence of a priest – but it is hard to conceive of a situation which would warrant anything comparable in the case of the Eucharist

5.15   The reason why baptism came to have this different status in relation to the ordained ministry is that in the case of baptism there was always the possibility of genuine emergency. No unbaptised person should be left to die while desiring baptism but beyond the reach of an ordained minister. In the case of the Eucharist, the question of 'emergency' did not arise because of the very early practice of reserving the eucharistic elements for the sick and dying, and because dying without the Eucharist has never been thought to jeopardise one's eternal salvation. The fact that this reasoning has often been motivated by what is widely seen today as a dubious anxiety about the eternal destiny of the unbaptised need not affect its force when considering who presides at the Eucharist. If baptism is about initiation into Christ and his Church, it makes no theological sense to refuse it in a near-death situation simply because of the absence of an ordained priest. In the case of the Eucharist, the sacrament of continuing nourishment and sustenance, the language of 'emergency' has of course been used by those who propose lay presidency, but it is hard to conceive of a situation which would warrant anything comparable to the practice of lay baptism in the context of the danger of death. This is not to give the Eucharist some higher status than baptism, nor vice versa; it is only to recognise the distinctive character of each.

Authorisation/licensing

supporters of lay presidency usually advocate, instead of ordination, some form of authorisation or licensing

5.16   Supporters of lay presidency usually advocate, instead of ordination, some form of authorisation or licensing of a local deacon or lay person to preside at the Eucharist, similar to the licensing of a lay Reader to preach. Various schemes have been suggested. The person chosen might be someone who is a natural leader or pastor of the community, or a licensed Reader, or some other respected layperson. (These three categories are not mutually exclusive; neither are they necessarily mutually inclusive.) Careful provisions have been suggested by some to take account of the approval of the local community, the bishop and minister; due preparation, including (in some cases) the insistence that the person must also be someone fit to preach (to ensure that word and sacrament are held together); special arrangements for deacons; and specification of the circumstances when it would be thought suitable for such a person to assume presidency.[8]

there are fundamental differences:

5.17   While acknowledging the care with which such arrangements are often set out, there are some fundamental differences between authorisation/licensing and ordination which, in the light of our arguments above, make linking the former with eucharistic presidency questionable.

the first concerns catholicity; the second concerns pastoral oversight

5.18   The first concerns catholicity. Licensing/authorisation in this model is the recognition of a person for a particular work in a particular community; it is limited as to duration, place and circumstances. Ordination is (potentially) unlimited in these respects for it is for service in the universal Church (see 3.29). At ordination a minister is placed in a special (and permanent) relationship to the Church as a whole. He or she will also be licensed to exercise his or her ministry in a particular locality and within certain constraints, thus giving expression in the local community to this special relationship to the whole Church, but this is not itself ordination. We have argued that at the Eucharist the local Church is united in a living and concentrated way with the catholic Church (4.11; 4.15); ordination would thus seem more fitting than licensing to link with eucharistic presidency.[9] The second difference concerns pastoral oversight. Authorisation to preside at the Eucharist is one thing; ordination to overall pastoral responsibility for a community is another. Eucharistic presidency, we have contended, properly flows out of the commission to pastoral oversight (4.45 –4.46). The third difference concerns the way in which each is conferred. Authorisation is a juridical act; ordination is first and foremost a liturgical act (though it includes juridical elements).[10] Eucharistic presidency is an event in the life of the Church which proceeds out of community oversight – the proper way to 'authorise' leaders of communities who will thus preside at the Eucharist is through the laying on of hands and prayer, i.e. through a liturgical event in the life of the Church rather than administrative procedure.

Deacons as presidents?

it could be argued that to authorise deacons to preside would confuse rather than clarify issues

5.19   The suggestion has sometimes been made that deacons might be authorised to preside at the Eucharist. However, it could be argued that to give such an authorisation would confuse rather than clarify issues concerning the diaconate and wider questions of ministry and order, both within the Anglican Church and in an ecumenical context. The 'Hanover Report' (1996) of the Anglican-Lutheran International Commission, *The Diaconate as Ecumenical*

Opportunity, explores diaconal ministry as a gift and potent symbol of servanthood in its own right, not as a presbyterate *manqué*. It makes the point[11] that because the diaconate is not burdened with problems of validity and canonical recognition – and, one might add, the question of eucharistic presidency – it provides an opportunity for a common ecumenically recognised ministry. Seen in these terms, the diaconate – whether permanent or 'transitional' – is distinct from the ministry of pastoral oversight in a particular place which a presbyter is called to share with the bishop and which is expressed in eucharistic presidency. A similar point could be made concerning the distinctiveness of 'licensed lay' reader ministry.[12]

6

Conclusion

the Eucharist is a feast in which we are drawn into the life of the Trinity

6.1   In this theological statement we have attempted to set the question of who presides at the Eucharist in its broadest context, the place of worship and mission of the Church within the purposes of the triune God. The Eucharist, we found, is a trinitarian feast in which we are drawn by grace into the very life of the Trinity, and in being drawn in are sent out to partake of the triune God's mission to the world.

the responsibilities of presidency are neither to be sought, nor to be guarded as a symbol of status

6.2   We can only speak with awe of presiding at such an act. We do not see it as an exclusive privilege to be jealously defended by an élite. George Herbert's Parson, when he came to the sacrament, was 'in great confusion, as being not only to receive God, but to break, and administer him.'[1] Tone and atmosphere matter to the life of the Church, and that is the authentic tone of reverence in the presence of a holy mystery. The responsibilities of presidency are neither to be sought, nor to be guarded as a symbol of status.

the ordinals of the Church of England show the seriousness of the lifelong commitment entailed in giving oneself to the office of priesthood

6.3   The wisdom of the Church over the centuries has been that the celebration of this holy feast should be prepared for with care. An aspect of that is the way in which its presidents are chosen, then trained, and then constantly nourished and supported in the life of priesthood. Examination of the ordinals of the Church of England shows the esteem in which the office is held, and the seriousness of the lifelong commitment entailed in giving oneself to it. A sermon at the ordination of priests is to declare 'how necessary that Order is in the Church of Christ, and also how the people ought to esteem them in their Office' (BCP Ordinal, rubric). The ordaining bishop states to the ordinands 'of what dignity, and of how great importance this Office is, whereunto ye be called', and requires that they should 'as much as lieth in you, ... apply yourselves wholly to this one thing, and draw all your cares and studies this way'. It is by the gracious gift of the Holy Spirit, not merely that 'various orders' have been appointed in Christ's one holy, catholic and apostolic Church, as the Ember collect states, but also that these orders are occupied by persons of humility, who heed the apostolic injunction to reckon others better than themselves (Philippians 2. 3), and who are eager to serve and do not lord it over the flock of God (1 Peter 5. 2-3).

we affirm and celebrate that tradition

6.4   Even in the greatly changed circumstances of the modern Church we find ourselves keen not merely to affirm that tradition, but to celebrate it. And in doing so we gladly speak in harmony with the vast majority of our ecumenical partners.

even if there is an apparent shortage of those who offer themselves for this office, God has already provided his Church with the resources to meet the situation

6.5   We have confidence that even if there is an apparent shortage of those who offer themselves for this office, God has already provided his Church with the resources to meet the situation. In our own context, which is increasingly that of primary mission, the development of non-stipendiary priesthood in ministries of various kinds is proving to be a creative development. These ministries meet such arguments in favour of lay presidency as are based on the shortage of priests. Where a community believes that it has been given by God a person with the requisite gifts for the priestly task, there exist ways and means by which the Church may test that identification, and the person once chosen may be trained for his or her demanding and sacrificial vocation. Ordination to priesthood in the Church of God is the publicly recognised mark of that call.

ordained ministries are a sign of the marks of the Church

6.6   But of all these ordained ministries we should want to affirm that they are, of their own nature, designed to be (and, please God, are) a sign of, and a means of drawing out, the marks of the Church, helping to bring about and realise in others the different ways in which the Church can participate in the priesthood of Christ and thus in the purposes of the triune God.

Notes

Notes to Chapter I

1 Clement 40.1. A translation appears in Staniforth (1968).

2 *The Theology of Ordination* (1975), cf. VIII, pars. 50ff.

3 The ASB rubrics make it clear that the president plays an active role at the crucial points that constitute the eucharistic assembly – including the opening greeting that signals the convening of the assembly. The saying of the greeting, for example, by a deacon or lay person, is permitted when necessity dictates (rubric, p. 115).

4 See below, 1.14.

5 Cf. 5.8 below.

6 The most relevant Articles are XXIII, XXVI, XXXVI. We should also note that Article XXXVII is careful to rebut the charge that 'ministering either of God's Word or of the Sacraments' is implied in the Royal Supremacy.

7 The relevant Canons are C1 and B12: see 1.4–1.9 above.

8 It is not clear precisely what 'consecrate' and 'administer' are intended to cover when used in the BCP and in Canon B12:1.

9 Attempts have been made to argue that exceptions were allowed to the general rule in the case of preaching and administering baptism and that therefore some English reformers would have accepted the propriety of lay presidency at the Eucharist. Cf. Beckwith (1964), pp. 42–6. This thesis has not found wide support, though it is certainly true that in the BCP baptism by a lay person is allowed in the case of an emergency.

10 *Laws*, Book V, LXXVII, 2.

11 See 'A Christian Letter' in Booty (1982), Vol IV, pp. 35–7.

12 Canon A5.

13 Cf. Cocksworth (1993).

14 Cf. also *God's Reign and Our Unity* (1984), par. 83.

15 *The Theology of Ordination* (1975), par. 54.

16 Tiller (1983), p. 120.

17 Harvey (1975), pp. 46–8.

18 Hargrave (1990).

19 Day (1995).

20 Marriage (1996).

21 *Extended Communion* (1993).

22 *Extended Communion* (1995).

23 *Many Gifts, One Spirit* (1987), p. 57.

24 *The Truth Shall Make You Free* (1988), par. 205.

25 The Principles and Recommendations, and the papers of the working groups (each of which was approved only by the group which prepared it) are gathered together in Holeton (1996).

26   Holeton (1996), p. 7.

27   Holeton (1996), p. 22.

28   Cf. *Lay Presidency at the Eucharist* (1995), pp. 54ff. See also the report of the Australian Doctrine Commission *Who may celebrate? Boundaries of Anglican Order* (1996), edited by Ivan Head.

29   Cf. Hargrave (1990).

30   Preface to the Declaration of Assent.

31   Cf. *The Final Report of ARCIC* (1982), 'Ministry and Ordination', par. 12, and its 'Elucidation', par. 2.

32   *The Fetter Lane Common Statement [Fetter Lane]*, 1996, paras. 31 and 36. In its schedule of issues still to be faced (par. 52), the text points to the need for a re-appraisal of the diaconate.

33   *The Manual* (1995), par. 24. The statement continues: 'The pastoral needs of each situation shall be reviewed periodically by the district council in consultation with the local Church. Apart from ordained ministers of the United Reformed Church and of other Churches, only such recognised persons may be invited.' In 1995, the General Assembly of the URC affirmed that 'in situations of pastoral necessity where no minister is available, the district council should make provision for lay presidency, normally from within the congregation concerned; elders and lay preachers should be considered first' and 'authorisation for lay presidency should not cover a period longer than a year without consultation and a review of the needs of the congregation concerned.' See also Anglican-Methodist dialogue below, n. 34.

34   *Commitment to Mission and Unity* (1996), par. 18, identifies the different positions held by the Church of England and the Methodist Church concerning the authorisation of lay persons to preside at the Eucharist as one of the issues which would need to be agreed in formal conversations.

35   Cf. e.g. *Baptism, Eucharist and Ministry* (1982), 'Ministry', par. 14; *The Final Report* (1982), 'Ministry and Ordination', par. 12, and its 'Elucidation', par. 2.

36   It should be borne in mind, nevertheless, that some of the strongest calls for lay presidency have arisen in circles of the Roman Catholic Church, where the shortage of clergy presents difficulties to some local communities. See e.g. Schillebeeckx (1981), Küng (1972), Boff (1986).

Notes to Chapter 2

1   *The Forgotten Trinity* (1989), p. 29.

2   *Episcopal Ministry* (1990), p. 8.

3   *God's Reign and Our Unity* (1984), par. 25.

4   *God's Reign and Our Unity* (1984), par. 27.

5   *The Meissen Common Statement [Meissen]* (1992), par. 3; *Porvoo* (1993), par. 20 and *Fetter Lane* (1996), par. 21.

6   *Church as Communion* (1991), par. 8.

7   Cf. e.g. *The Final Report of ARCIC I* (1982), *Introduction; Church as Communion* (1991); McDonnell (1988); Tillard (1992); Evans (1994); Avis (1990); Zizioulas (1985). See also *Meissen* (1992), paras. 4–5; *Porvoo* (1993), paras. 15–18; *Fetter Lane* (1996), paras. 22–3.

8   *Church as Communion* (1991), par. 3.

9   Cf. Congar (1983), pp. 5–14; *Zizioulas* (1985), Ch. 3.

10 *The Forgotten Trinity* (1989), p. 29. See also *Porvoo* (1993), paras. 19 and 38.

11 Cf. Land (1993).

12 *Porvoo* (1993), par. 23.

13 For a discussion of the four marks of the Church, see the Anglican/Orthodox *Dublin Agreed Statement* (1984), paras. 8–17.

14 For a discussion of the eschatological character of each of the four marks of the Church, see *Church as Communion* (1991) paras. 25–41.

Notes to Chapter 3

1   *God's Reign and Our Unity* (1984), par. 74.

2   *The Mystery of Salvation* (1995), p. 136.

3   Avis (1981), p. 95.

4   The point is made concisely in *Baptism, Eucharist and Ministry* (1990), M17.

5   *All Are Called* (1985).

6   '*The primary location of the laity is in society at large.* It is important that the clergy and lay officials of the Church should understand and respect the truth that most laity are only *secondarily* located in the institutional Church.' *All Are Called* (1985), p. 67.

7   Cf. *The Theology of Ordination* (1975), par. 8.

8   *God's Reign and Our Unity* (1984), par. 77.

9   *The Final Report* (1982), 'Ministry and Ordination', par. 5.

10 *The Final Report* (1982), 'Ministry and Ordination', par. 5.

11 On the change of the pattern of episcopate from local to regional, see *Niagara* (1987), paras. 42ff.

12 *Meissen*, par. 15 (ix).

13 'The threefold ministry of bishop, presbyter and deacon may serve as an expression of the unity we seek and also as a means for achieving it.' *Baptism, Eucharist and Ministry* (1982), 'Ministry', par. 22.

14 *God's Reign and Our Unity* (1984), paras. 94–6.

15 *Schillebeeckx* (1981).

16 Cf. *Greenwood* (1994), Ch. 1.

17 *Porvoo* (1993), par. 32, j; cf. *Meissen* (1992), par. 15 (viii).

18 Cf. the *Second Helvetic Confession*, 1566: 'To be sure, Christ's apostles call all who believe in Christ "priests", but not on account of an office, but because, all the faithful having been made kings and priests, we are able to offer up spiritual sacrifices to God through Christ. Therefore, the priesthood and ministry are very different from one another. For the priesthood, as we have just said, is common to all Christians; not so is the ministry.' Quoted by J. N. Collins (1992), p. 25.

19 Cf. e.g. *The Theology of Ordination* (1975): 'the ordained ministry acts as an articulating focus for the total life of the priestly body of the Church' (par. 46); *The Priesthood of the Ordained Ministry* (1986), par. 120.

20 The language of some ecumenical agreement is that of 'divine institution' (e.g. *Porvoo* (1993), par. 32, j.; cf. *Meissen* (1992), par. 15 (viii)).

21 Cf. *Ordination and the Church's Ministry* (1991), pp. 36ff.

22 In speaking of the relation of Christ to the ordained priest, a large cluster of terms have been used – e.g. 'image', 'type', 'icon,' etc. The priest has also been spoken of as in (or *ex) persona Christi*, or *in nomine Christi*. Aquinas speaks of the minister as *in virtute Christi*: that is to say, the priest acts but only in virtue of Christ. We believe the phrase 'in the name of Christ' presents fewest difficulties.

23 So Canon C.1, 2: 'No person who has been admitted to the order of bishop, priest or deacon can ever be divested of the character of his order'. This term is defended by Richard Hooker in virtue of the 'power of the ministry of God', bestowed at ordination (*Laws*, Book V, LXXVII, 2). By Eric Mascall and other modern writers the permanence of ordination is seen in terms of relation rather than quality. Cf. Mascall (1977), pp. 211–31.

24 *God's Reign and Our Unity* (1984), paras. 85, 86.

25 From the examination of Deacons and Priests in the BCP Ordinal.

26 On 'local', cf. 1.13.

27 *Apostolicity and Succession* (1994), par. 11; cf. *Church as Communion* (1991), par. 32; *Porvoo* (1993), par. 39.

28 *Porvoo* (1993), par. 51.

29 *Apostolicity and Succession* (1994), par. 56.

30 *Apostolicity and Succession* (1994), paras. 57–67; *Porvoo* (1993), paras. 52, 53.

Notes to Chapter 4

1 See also the trinitarian understanding of the Eucharist as expressed in *Baptism, Eucharist and Ministry* (1990).

2 The theological theme of 'remembering' has a strong background in Jewish thought, and the Hebrew root *zkr* has rich associations of meanings: not only to recall, but to remember in such a way that the past is felt to impinge directly on the present, and hope is renewed for the future.

3 Heron (1983), p. 169.

4 *Meissen* (1992), par. 15 (v). The literature on these issues is voluminous, and much ecumenical energy has been directed towards the search for sensitive and nuanced articulation of the notion of the Eucharist as our offering.

5 Cf. Romans 15. 16 and Philippians 2. 16, 17 where the language of sacrifice is related to evangelism.

6 Heron (1983), p. 54, italics omitted.

7 McPartlan (1995), p. 6.

8   See also *Baptism, Eucharist and Ministry* (1990), par. 20.

9   From one of the group statements of IALC–5; Holeton (1996), p. 18. Cf. also 2.4–2.19 above.

10   From one of the group statements of IALC–5; Holeton (1996), p. 9.

11   *God's Reign and Our Unity* (1984), par. 64.

12   Conzelmann (1975), p. 172.

13   The Swiss Reformer, Zwingli, drew on one of the ancient meanings of 'sacrament' (*sacramentum*) and spoke of the Eucharist as a sign of one's membership of the Church. The faithful attenders are like the loyal soldiers gathered around the regimental standard bearer. In a similar way, the Parish Communion movement, with its slogan – 'the Lord's people around the Lord's Table on the Lord's Day' – saw the Eucharist as a sign of the gathering of God's people.

14   *Baptism, Eucharist and Ministry* (1982), 'Eucharist', par. 19.

15   This is not to suggest a localised presence of Christ in an exclusive sense, in the sacrament or its elements; cf. Cranfield (1965): 'there is a real presence of the exalted Christ in the persons of his brethren in their need and distress comparable with his real presence in the Word and Sacraments...', p. 28.

16   See further at 5.12–5.13 below.

17   It is possible that Hebrews is regularly alluding to the Eucharist.

18   Holeton (1996), p. 7. The term 'concelebration' was once used for this and, arguably, ought to be restored, thus rescuing it from its modern and distorted sense of 'consecration by simultaneous presidential recitation'.

19   Holeton (1996), p. 20.

20   P. Bradshaw (1983), pp. 6ff; Rajak and Noy (1993).

21   Augustine (354–430) is a case in point. The involvement of the entire community in the Eucharist is fundamental for Augustine. He wanted every believer to know that the whole body of the Church has a priesthood entrusted to it. The laity are as much called to service as the clergy. The ordained minister is a representative, not a substitute or mediator between God and people – his work and prayer are not to be seen as where the real action of the Church occurs while the laity are mere spectators. But at the same time, Augustine took it as self-evident that lay people could not preside at the Eucharist, even in an emergency.

22   See his treatise *De Exhortatione Castitatis* discouraging polygamy, the work which includes the statement (7.3) 'where there are no clergy ... you are your own priest [*sacerdos es tibi solus*], for where two or three are gathered together, there is the Church, even if these three are lay people.'

23   Sociological factors and changing attitudes may have influenced developments in patterns of ministry: cf. para. 1.40 above.

24   P. Bradshaw (1983), pp. 9ff.

25   The most important source for Luther's treatment of these matters is *Appeal to the Christian Nobility of the German Nation* (1520) in Luther (1888).

26   Cranmer, *On the Lord's Supper*, Book V:11.

27   Cf. e.g. *The Final Report* (1982), 'Ministry and Ordination', par. 12; *The Ministry in the Church* (1981), par. 31; *Baptism, Eucharist and Ministry* (1982), 'Ministry', par. 14.

28   Holeton (1996), p. 7.

29   Holeton (1996), p. 19.

Notes to Chapter 5

1   *God's Reign and Our Unity* (1984), par. 83.

2   Lloyd (1977), p. 9.

3   Buchanan (1996), p. 2.

4   Cf. Chapter 3 above, especially 3.20–3.37. It is also important to recognise that emerging forms of ministry make it increasingly likely that pastoral responsibility will be entrusted to teams, perhaps including lay ministers as well as priests, rather than a single ordained person in each place. While the bishop's oversight expressed as pastoral care can be very widely shared with lay people, it remains true that his sacramental responsibilities are shared with particular people set aside for it by ordination.

5   Holeton (1996), p. 22.

6   This, of course, raises many questions about ordination training, but this is beyond the confines of this report.

7   It is worth recalling that the initial reluctance in the Church of England to allow Readers to preach was motivated less by clericalism than by a concern to hold together the ministry of word and sacrament.

8   Cf. e.g. *Lay Presidency at the Eucharist* (1995), pp. 57ff.

9   It has been suggested that recognising certain lay persons as possible eucharistic presidents should be officially described as a 'temporary ordination'. For the reasons we have set out, we find this unacceptable. Cf. above, 3.29 and n. 23.

10   Interestingly, as Paul Gibson points out, there is a tendency among the proponents of lay presidency to take refuge in a very high doctrine of episcopacy 'in which the bishop's juridical acts (e.g., licensing) are made equal to the bishop's liturgical acts (e.g., ordination).' Paul Gibson, in Talley (1988), p. 35.

11   Conclusion, par. 79.

12   See also *Fetter Lane*, 1996 and 1.33–1.39 above.

Note to Chapter 6

13   Herbert, *A Priest to the Temple*, Ch. XXII, 'The Parson in Sacraments'.

Bibliography

Dialogue texts

(i)   Anglican–Lutheran

Anglican–Lutheran Dialogue, the Report of the European Commission, SPCK, 1983.

Anglican–Lutheran Relations, Report of the Anglican–Lutheran Joint Working Group, ACC, 1983.

Report of the Anglican–Lutheran Consultation on Episkope, *The Niagara Report* [*Niagara*], CHP, 1987.

The Diaconate as Ecumenical Opportunity: the Hanover Report of the Anglican–Lutheran International Commission, [Hanover], Anglican Communion Publications, 1996.

(ii)   Anglican–Orthodox

Anglican–Orthodox Dialogue, *The Moscow Agreed Statement*, SPCK, 1977.

Anglican–Orthodox Dialogue, *The Dublin Agreed Statement*, SPCK, 1984.

(iii)   Anglican–Reformed

God's Reign and Our Unity, the Report of the Anglican–Reformed International Commission, SPCK, 1984.

(iv)   Anglican–Roman Catholic

The Final Report (of ARCIC I), CTS/SPCK, 1982.

Church as Communion, an Agreed Statement by the Second Anglican–Roman Catholic International Commission, CTS/CHP, 1991.

Life in Christ: Morals, Communion and the Church, an Agreed Statement by the Second Anglican–Roman Catholic International Commission, CTS/CHP, 1994.

(v)   Lutheran–Roman Catholic

The Malta Report, 1972.

Ways to Community, 1980.

The Ministry in the Church, 1981.

These reports can be found in *Growth in Agreement* (1984) (see **Books and articles** below).

(vi)   Methodist–Roman Catholic

The Denver Report, 1972.

The Dublin Report, 1977.

The Honolulu Report, 1981.

These reports can be found in *Growth in Agreement* (1984) (see **Books and articles** below).

Towards a Statement on the Church, WMC, 1986.

The Apostolic Tradition, WMC, 1991.

(vii) Anglican–Moravian

Anglican–Moravian Conversations. *The Fetter Lane Common Statement with essays in Moravian and Anglican history [Fetter Lane]*, CCU, 1996.

(viii) Multilateral texts

Baptism, Eucharist and Ministry [The *Lima* Text], Faith and Order Paper 111, WCC, 1982.

Churches Respond to Baptism, Eucharist and Ministry, vols I–VI, WCC, 1984–86.

Baptism, Eucharist and Ministry, 1982–1990, WCC, 1990.

Regional reports

Towards Full Communion and Concordat of Agreement, Lutheran–Episcopal Dialogue USA, W. A. Norgren and W. G. Rusch (eds), Forward Movement Publications, 1991.

The Meissen Common Statement [Meissen], in *The Meissen Agreement Texts*, CCU, 1992.

Together in Mission and Ministry, the Porvoo Common Statement [Porvoo], Conversations between the British and Irish Anglican Churches and Nordic and Baltic–Lutheran Churches, CHP, 1993.

Papers and reports of the Church of England and General Synod

All Are Called: Toward a Theology of the Laity, CIO, 1985.

Apostolicity and Succession, General Synod, 1994 (GS, Misc 432).

Call to Order: Vocation and Ministry in the Church of England, ACCM, 1989.

Commitment to Mission and Unity, the Report of the Informal Conversations between the Methodist Church and the Church of England, CHP/Methodist Publishing House, 1996 (GS Misc 477).

Episcopal Ministry, the Report of the Archbishops' Group on the Episcopate, CHP, 1990.

Extended Communion, General Synod, 1993 (GS1082).

Extended Communion, General Synod, 1995 (GS Misc 452).

Ordination and the Church's Ministry: a Theological Evaluation, Central Board of Finance of the Church of England, 1991.

The Priesthood of the Ordained Ministry, BMU, 1986 (GS 694).

The Reconciliation of Ministries, CIO, 1977 (GS 307).

The Theology of Ordination, CIO, 1975 (GS 281).

Towards a Church of England Response to BEM & ARCIC, CIO, 1985 (GS 661).

Books and articles

Avis, Paul, *Christians in Communion*, Chapman, 1990.

Avis, Paul, *The Church in the Theology of the Reformers*, Marshall, Morgan and Scott, 1981.

Baxter, Christina, 'Leadership in the Church of England', in Gordon Kuhrt (ed.), *To Proclaim Afresh: Evangelical Agenda for the Church*, SPCK, 1995, pp. 36–59.

Baxter, Christina (ed.), *Stepping Stones*, Hodder & Stoughton, 1987.

Beckwith, Roger, *Priesthood and Sacraments: a Study in the Anglican–Methodist Report*, Marcham Manor Press, 1964.

Boff, Leonardo, *Ecclesiogenesis*, Collins, 1986.

Booty, J. E. (ed.), *The Works of Richard Hooker, vol. IV, 'Of the Laws of Ecclesiastical Polity: Attack and Response'*, Cambridge MA, 1982.

Bradshaw, Paul, *Liturgical Presidency in the Early Church*, Grove, 1983.

Bradshaw, Paul, *The Anglican Ordinal*, SPCK, 1971.

Bradshaw, Paul, '"*Ubi eucharistia, ibi ecclesia*": Ecclesiological Reflections on Ministry, Order and Eucharist', unpublished paper delivered at the International Anglican Liturgical Consultation, Dublin, 1995.

Bradshaw, Tim, *The Olive Branch*, Paternoster, 1992.

Buchanan, Colin, 'Editorial', in *News of Liturgy*, 253 (Jan. 1996), pp. 1–3.

Card, T., *Priesthood in Crisis*, SCM, 1988.

Carr, Wesley, *The Priestlike Task: a Model for Training and Developing the Church's Ministry*, SPCK, 1985

Cocksworth, Christopher, *Evangelical Eucharistic Thought in the Church of England*, CUP, 1993.

Collins, J.N., *Are all Christians Ministers?* E.J. Dwyer, 1992.

Collins, Mary, & Power, David (eds), *Can We Always Celebrate the Eucharist? Concilium*, T & T Clark, 1982.

Congar, Yves, *I Believe in the Holy Spirit*, vol. 2, Seabury, 1983.

Conzelmann, Hans, *I Corinthians*, Fortress Press, 1975.

Cranfield, C. E. B., *The Service of God*, Epworth Press, 1965.

Cranmer, Thomas, *Defence of the True and Catholic Doctrine of the Sacrament*, 1550, reprinted in James Packer and Gervase Duffield (eds), *The Work of Thomas Cranmer*, Sutton Courtenay Press, 1964.

Day, David, 'The Ministry of Laity', in Charles Yeats (ed.), *Has Keele Failed? Reform in the Church of England*, Hodder & Stoughton, 1995, pp. 104–16.

Drilling, P., *Trinity and Ministry*, Fortress, 1991.

Eastwood, C., *The Priesthood of All Believers*, Epworth, 1960.

Evans, G. R., *The Church and the Churches*, CUP, 1994.

Faivre, Alexandre, *The Emergence of the Laity in the Church*, Paulist Press, 1990.

Forte, B., *The Church: Icon of the Trinity*, St Paul, 1991.

Gills, Kevin, *What on Earth is the Church? A Biblical and Theological Inquiry*, SPCK, 1995.

Green, H. Benedict, *Lay Presidency at the Eucharist*, Darton, Longman and Todd, 1994.

Greenwood, Robin, *Transforming Priesthood: a New Theology of Mission and Ministry*, SPCK, 1994.

Griffins, James E. & Martens, Daniel F. (eds), *A Commentary on 'Concordat of Agreement'*, Augsburg Fortress, 1994.

Growth in Agreement, Reports and Agreed Statements of Ecumenical Conversations on a World Level, Harding Meyer and Lukas Vischer (eds), WCC, 1984.

Gunton, C., *The Promise of Trinitarian Theology*, T & T Clark, 1989.

Hanson, R., *Christian Priesthood Examined*, Lutterworth, 1979.

Hargrave, Alan, *But Who Will Preside?* Grove, 1990.

Harvey, A. E., *Priest or President?* SPCK, 1975.

Heron, Alasdair, *Table and Tradition: Towards an Ecumenical Understanding of the Eucharist*, Handsel Press, 1983.

Holeton, David R., *Renewing the Anglican Eucharist: Findings of the Fifth International Anglican Liturgical Consultation, Dublin, Eire, 1995*, Grove, 1996.

Hooker, William, *Of the Lawes of Ecclesiastical Politie*, Book V, 1597.

James, Paul, *Liturgical Presidency*, Grove, 1993.

Kruse, Colin, *New Testament Foundations for Ministry*, Marshall Morgan & Scott, 1983.

Küng, H., *Why Priests?* Fontana, 1972.

LaCugna, C. M., *God For Us*, Harper Collins, 1991.

Land, Steven, 'Pentecostal Spirituality: a Passion for the Kingdom', *Journal of Pentecostal Theology*, 1 (1993), pp. 19–46.

Lay Presidency at the Eucharist: a Theological Consultation, Standing Committee of General Synod of the Anglican Church of Australia, 1995.

Legrand, Hervé-Marie, 'The Presidency of the Eucharist in the Ancient Church', *Worship*, 27 (1979), pp. 413–38.

Lloyd, Trevor, *Lay Presidency at the Eucharist?* Grove, 1977.

Luther, Martin, *Appeal to the Christian Nobility of the German Nation* (1520), in *D. Martin Luthers Werke: Kritische Gesamtausgabe*, vol. 6, Böhlau, 1888, pp. 404–69.

McDonnell, Kilian, 'Vatican 2 (1962–1964), Pueblo (1979), Synod (1985): *Koinonia/Communio* as an Integral Ecclesiology', *Journal of Ecumenical Studies*, 25 (1988), pp. 399–427.

McPartlan, Paul, *Sacrament of Salvation: an Introduction to Eucharistic Ecclesiology*, T & T Clark, 1995.

McPartlan, Paul, *The Eucharist Makes the Church. Henri de Lubac and John Zizioulas in Dialogue*, T & T Clark, 1993.

Many Gifts, One Spirit, Report of ACC–7, ACC, 1987.

Marriage, Alwyn, *The People of God: a Royal Priesthood*, DLT, 1996.

Mascall, E. L., *Theology and the Gospel of Christ: an Essay in Reorientation*, SPCK, 1977.

Moberly, R., *Ministerial Priesthood*, Murray, 1899.

Moltmann, J., *The Church in the Power of the Spirit*, SCM, 1977.

Neill, Stephen, *Anglicanism*, Mowbray, 1977.

Rajak, Tessa & Noy, David, '*Archisynagogoi*: Office, Title and Social Status in the Greco-Jewish Synagogue', *Journal of Roman Studies*, 83 (1993), pp. 75–93.

Richardson, Alan, *An Introduction to the Theology of the New Testament*, SCM, 1958.

Rordorf, Willy, *The Eucharist of the Early Christians*, Pueblo, 1978.

Schillebeeckx, E., *Ministry*, SCM, 1981.

Staniforth, Maxwell (tr.), *Early Christian Writings*, Penguin, 1968.

Stevenson, Kenneth, *Covenant of Grace Renewed*, DLT, 1994.

Sykes, S., *The Integrity of Anglicanism*, Mowbray, 1978.

Sykes, S. & Booty, J. (eds), *The Study of Anglicanism*, SPCK, 1988.

Talley, Thomas J., *A Kingdom of Priests: Liturgical Formation of the People of God*, Grove, 1988.

Tertullian, *Quinti Septimii Florentis Tertulliani quae supersunt omnia*, ed. F. Oehler, Weigel, 1993.

The Forgotten Trinity: I – The Report of the BCC Study Commission of Trinitarian Doctrine Today, British Council of Churches, 1989

The Manual, United Reformed Church in the United Kingdom, 1995.

The Truth Shall Make You Free: the Reports, Resolutions and Pastoral Letters from the Bishops, CHP, 1988.

Thurian, Max, *Ecumenical Perspectives on BEM*, WCC, 1983.

Tillard, J. M., *Church of Churches: the Ecclesiology of Communion*, Glazier, 1992.

Tillard, J. M., *What Priesthood has the Ministry?* Grove, 1973.

Tiller, John, *A Strategy for the Church's Ministry*, CIO, 1983.

Zizioulas, J., *Being as Communion*, Darton, Longman and Todd, 1985.